Visible Signs

Fairchild Books
An imprint of Bloomsbury Publishing Plc

Imprint previously known as AVA Publishing

50 Bedford Square
London
WC1B 3DP
UK

1385 Broadway
New York
NY 10018
USA

www.bloomsbury.com

FAIRCHILD BOOKS, BLOOMSBURY
and the Diana logo are trademarks of
Bloomsbury Publishing Plc

British Library Cataloguing-in-Publication Data
A catalogue record for this book is available from
the British Library.

ISBN: PB: 978-1-4742-3242-5
       ePDF: 978-1-4742-3244-9

Library of Congress Cataloging-in-Publication
Data

Crow, David, 1962-
Visible Signs : an introduction to semiotics in the
visual arts / David Crow. — Third edition.
pages cm. — (Required reading range)
ISBN 978-1-4742-3242-5 (paperback) — ISBN
978-1-4742-3244-9 (epdfs) 1. Semiotics.
2. Semiotics and art. 3. Visual communication.
I. Title.
P99.C77 2016
302.2—dc23
2015006998

Visible Signs
An Introduction
to Semiotics in the
Visual Arts
By David Crow

Fairchild Books
An imprint of Bloomsbury Publishing Plc

BLOOMSBURY
LONDON · NEW DELHI · NEW YORK · SYDNEY

TABLE OF CONTENTS

Jetzt

WATERPROOF

Waterproof fabric, sealed seams.

WINDPROOF

BREATHAE

PICTURE ADJUSTMENT CARD

Swing the Loop Antenna back and forth,
sideways for optimum reception.

SONY CORPORAT

Printed in Japan©

4-498-264-11 (1)

S

C

4-498-264-11 (1)

Printed in Japan©

SONY CORPORAT

ASSEMBLY INSTRUCTIO

1. When you look at your card you will see that
several different dinosaur model pieces and that each
a slot/s cut into it. The slots are followed by a narrow sl
marked with a letter. You will find that there are two slot
with each letter, i.e. two slots with letter A, two with lette

2. Match up the letters, i.e. slot A fits into slot A, slot B
etc. Make sure you slide the pieces together tightly
end of both slits are touching and the connection
(See diagram below)

SLIT

SLIT

CUT

Introduction

This third edition of *Visible Signs* aims to explore the mechanics of visual language in an attempt to explain how visual communication works. The terms and theories used to explain visual communication are borrowed from linguistics (the study of language) and semiotics (the study of signs). The presentation of semiotic theory is often clouded by difficult language, which, in practice, makes the discussion of work unnecessarily challenging. This book is intended to help students unpack the signs in their own work, understand how communication works, and, if necessary, deconstruct their own work to determine why it is not working as they intended.

"Except for the immediate satisfaction of biological needs, man lives in a world not of things but of symbols." [1]

1. **L. Von Bertalanffy,** *General System Theory* *(George Braziller, Inc., 1968); quoted in D. Bolinger, Language: The Loaded Weapon (Longman, 1980).*

Michel Foucault

Charles Peirce

Roland Barthes

Ferdinand de Saussure

Gilles Deleuze

Jacques Derrida

Each chapter provides an overview of a particular facet of semiotic theory. The core text remains unchanged as it deals with well-established ideas and theories that are still relevant today. This edition updates the visual reference material in the portfolio pages with carefully selected examples of "real" design presented alongside extended captions. These function as mini case studies that refer explicitly to theories introduced in preceding chapters, illustrating the timeless nature of the underlying theories.

Many artists and designers find it difficult to explore theoretical material in academic writing. Each chapter ends with a series of short exercises that will help to ensure understanding of the ideas in Visible Signs through practical application. It is often easier to translate our thoughts and ideas into words by reflecting on experiences we have had or things we have made. The motivation behind this publication is to help students of art and design find credibility in their practice through a deeper understanding of many of the intuitive decisions they make.

1. Components

We begin our journey through semiotics by looking at the fundamental building blocks of language. Structuralists developed ideas and theories that demonstrated the arbitrary nature of language and determined the necessary formal conditions for languages to exist and develop. The study of art and design has borrowed heavily from these ideas, and here we begin to relate these to a visual language that uses both text and image.

2. How Meaning Is Formed

Having looked at the underlying structure of language and the sign, we examine how we extract meaning from a sign. We define the different categories of signs and discuss the structural relationships between them. We look at why some signs appear to be quite abstract and why these are still easily read and understood. We discuss how signs are organized into systems and how these underlying structures and patterns help to form meaning.

3. Reading the Sign

The transfer of meaning from author to reader is not a one-way process, but a process of creative exchange between author and reader. We introduce Roland Barthes' idea that semiotics takes in any system of signs, and the idea of a visual language. This chapter moves through a number of theoretical terms, helping us to appreciate the several layers of meaning in a sign and to understand how the reader interprets the way a sign is expressed.

4. Text and Image

This chapter continues with Roland Barthes' ideas about the relationship between text and image. He uses popular culture as a reference point to explain that these different types of signs have distinct structural relationships that can be employed by artists and designers to help control the way that their compositions are read.

5. Official and Unofficial Language

Language is a social and political instrument as well as a functional one. As languages are developed, a sense of hierarchy is also developed around those languages. This chapter looks at cultural hierarchy and examines the ways that societies ensure the acceptance and legitimization of language within their territorial boundaries. Outside of the recognized and approved use of visual language, there is a way of generating meaning that is independent of such political control. Here we explore the unofficial and informal codes that are used in daily life by many groups in our societies.

6. Symbolic Creativity

Visible Signs looks for the possibility of a visual language that already exists, growing from its own resources and used by a large group of people who could be said to be outside of the arts and media. This might be considered an informal visual language that does not use the economic field as its source of rationale. We will discuss the notion of symbolic creativity and its use by individuals to find ways of visually representing their identities.

7. Junk and Culture

We can identify a system by looking at what has been discarded from the system and classified as dirt or rubbish. We investigate the classification of cultural objects and look at the possibility of changing their value by placing them in an entirely different context. Here we also look at the use of rubbish as a resource for the visual arts. It allows artists and designers to bring new meaning to discarded items and explore alternative ways of creating meaning.

8. Open Work

The work of Umberto Eco is a key resource for exploring the creative relationship between author and audience. Here we explain the connection between communication and information; we explore how communication can be enriched by carefully creating the freedom for readers to make their own creative associations.

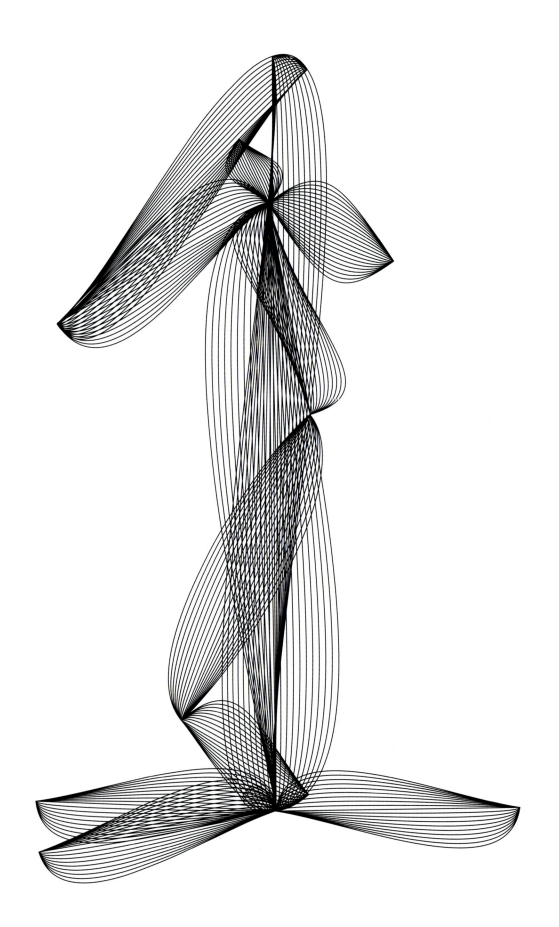

Chapter One
Components

What Is Theory?

The word "theory" comes from the Greek word *theoria,* meaning to view, to observe or to reflect. The dictionary defines theory as an explanation or system of anything: an exposition of the abstract principles of either a science or an art. Theory is a speculation on something rather than a practice.

1839 – 1914

Charles Pierce
Ferdinand de Saussure

1857 – 1913

The theories that we apply to graphic design and visual communication are taken from a study of the general science of signs known in Europe as semiology and in the United States as semiotics.

Saussure and Peirce

This new science was proposed in the early 1900s by Ferdinand de Saussure (1857–1913), a Swiss professor of linguistics. At around the same time, American philosopher Charles Sanders Peirce (1839–1914) was developing a parallel study of signs that he called semiotics. To avoid confusion, we will use the term *semiotics* as it has become more widely known. Although they were working independently, there were a number of fundamental similarities in their studies. Both Saussure and Peirce saw the sign as central to their studies. Both were primarily concerned with structural models of the sign, which concentrated on the relationship between the components of the sign.

For both Saussure and Peirce, it is this relationship between the components of the sign that enables us to turn signals, in whatever form they appear, into a message that we can understand. Although they used different terminology, there are clear parallels between the two descriptions of these models (see the diagram on p. 23).

However, there are also key differences between the studies. The most significant difference is that Saussure's was exclusively a linguistic study; as a result, he showed little interest in the part that the reader plays in the process. This was a major part of Peirce's model, as we shall see in the next chapter when we look at how meaning is formed. There are three main areas that form what we understand as semiotics: the signs themselves, the way they are organized into systems, and the context in which they appear. The underlying principles, which have become the cornerstone of modern semiotics, were first heard by students of Saussure in a course in linguistics at the University of Geneva between 1906 and 1911. Saussure died in 1913 without publishing his theories, and it was not until 1915 that the work was published by his students as the *Cours de Linguistique Générale* (*Course in General Linguistics*).

Prior to this, the study of language (linguistics) largely concerned itself with historical usage of languages. In the search for the source of meaning, linguists looked to the origins of language. Linguists supposed that if meaning could be found in language, then the nature of thought itself could be found by looking at the origins of language. In its early stages, linguistics was an attempt to explain signs by imagining them as descriptions of a series of gestures, actions, and sensations. This developed into a comparative study of the forms of words in different languages and their evolution. At this stage, linguists were concerned with the structure of language in its own right, with no distinct relation to the mind. Prior to assuming his post at Geneva, Saussure himself was concerned with the study of historical languages and had a particular interest in the comparative grammar of Indo-European languages, particularly Sanskrit.

Saussure was unhappy with the way linguists were approaching language, as he felt they had not determined the nature of what they were studying. As a result, Saussure proposed an entirely different way of looking at language, by returning to the essentials and looking at language as a system of signs. If we could understand how the system of language works, then this might lead us to how meaning is formed. One crucial difference in this approach was that Saussure and the structuralists were concerned with the underlying principles of language, which all speakers or bearers of a language have in common. These underlying principles are fixed and do not evolve over time with social or technological change. Saussure was a linguist. As a result, his theory focused on language and his model is centered on words as signs.

1.1
Saussure's Model for a Sign.

The two fundamental elements that make up a sign are the "signifier" and the "signified."
A sign is produced when these two elements are brought together.

1.1

Ferdinand de Saussure

There are three main areas that form what we understand as semiotics: the signs themselves, the way they are organized into systems, and the context in which they appear.

1.2
Crosses.

A variety of different crosses. The meaning of each cross is dependent on its context. (a) The Red Cross. (b) No smoking (c) The Cross of St. Nicholas. (d) Do not wring. (e) Hazardous chemical. (f) Positive Terminal. (g) The Cross of St.Sebastian. (h) The cross of St.Julian. (i) The cross of St.George. (j) No stopping sign (UK). (k) The cross of St.Nicholas. (l) The cross of St.Andrew

1.2

Linguistic Signs

According to Saussure, language is constructed from a small set of units called phonemes. These are the sounds that we use in a variety of combinations to construct words. These noises can only be judged as language when they attempt to communicate an idea. To do this, they must be part of a system of signs. The meaning of the individual units (the phonemes), which make up language, has been sacrificed in order to give a limitless number of meanings on a higher level as they are reassembled to form words. The word "dog," for example, has three phonemes: d, o, and g. In written form, the letters "d," "o," and "g" represent the sounds. In turn, these words then represent objects or, more accurately, a mental picture of objects.

What Saussure outlined is a system of representation. In this system, a letter—for example, the letter "d"—can represent a sound. A collection of letters (a word) is used to represent an object. Each of these examples contains the two fundamental elements that make up a sign: the signifier and the signified. A word became known as a signifier, and the object it represented became the signified. A sign is produced when these two elements are brought together. In different languages, the collection of phonemes that make up the signifier are different. In English-speaking countries, our four-legged friend is called a dog, whereas in France it is "chien," in Spain "perro," in Italy "cane," and in Germany "Hund." What this shows us is that the relationship between the signifier "dog" and the thing signified is a completely arbitrary one. Neither the sounds nor their written form bears any relation to the thing itself. With few exceptions, any similarity is accidental. Just as the letter "d" bears no relation to the sound we associate with it, the word used to describe a dog bears no relation to the thing it represents. Just as there is nothing book-like in the word "book," the word "dog" does not bite, the word "gun" cannot kill you, and the word "pipe" does not resemble the object used to smoke tobacco. This divorce between meaning and form is called duality.

cot clog crocus
cannon cross crow
collar calf dog

signified

sign

signifier

From an early age we are taught the relationship between the signifier and the signified. This is not something we are conscious of, but it remains one of the most fundamental building blocks in the structure of language.

"Duality freed concept and symbol from each other to the extent that change could now modify one without affecting the other."[2]

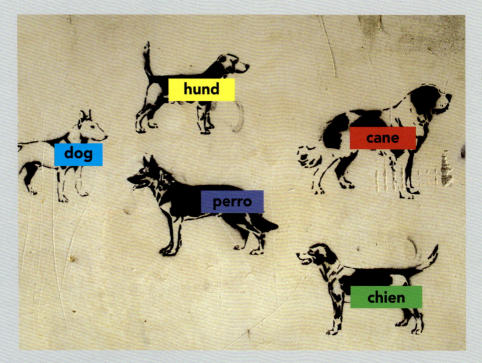

this is a dog

this is a copy

this is a scan

this is arbitrary

In English-speaking countries, our four-legged friend is called a dog, whereas in France it is "chien," in Spain "perro," in Italy "cane" and in Germany it is "Hund." What this shows us is that the relationship between the signifier "dog" and the thing signified is a completely arbitrary one.

Agreement

All that is necessary for any language to exist is an agreement amongst a group of people that one thing will stand for another.

There are two exceptions to this rule, but the fact that we can readily identify them as exceptions only reinforces the overriding rule that ordinary signs are constructed from arbitrary relationships. There are onomatopoeic words that in some way imitate the things they represent through the sounds they make. A dog, for example, could be described as a "bow-wow," a gun as a "bang-bang."

The second exception is where the sequence of sounds that make up the word or signifier is constructed from two separate signs, which might describe an action or the construction of the object it represents. A keyboard, for example, describes the object used for typing words. It is quite literally a board that holds the keys. However, this type of second-order signifier is only of use in English and does not transfer to other languages. A keyboard in English is "teclado" in Spanish. So we can see that the relationship between the sound and the thing it represents is learned. It is its use in social practice that helps us to understand its meaning.

Saussure also pointed out that language is not just a set of names chosen at random and attached to objects or ideas. We cannot simply replace the arbitrary name for one object in one language with the name in another language. Where English uses the word "key" to represent something that we press to type, turn to open a door, play on a piano, or use to describe a significant idea or moment—all from the same signifier—the translation into French would throw up a range of different words. Similarly, there are signifiers in one language that have no direct translation into other forms of language. Each language has a series of arbitrary signifiers that exist independently of any other language or dialect. Languages do not just find names for objects and ideas that are already categorized; languages define their own categories.

All that is necessary for any language to exist is an agreement among a group of people that one thing will stand for another. Furthermore, these agreements can be made quite independently of agreements in other communities. Saussure proposed that this was true of any language or dialect.

1.3

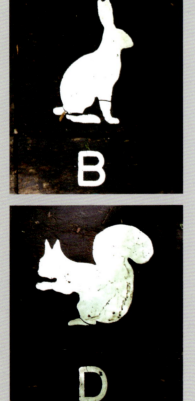

1.3
B for Rabbit,
D for Squirrel.

The confusion of being confronted by signifiers in an unfamiliar language

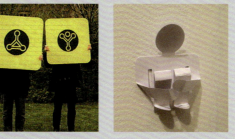

1.4

1.4
Man and Woman.

Different versions of signs for man and woman.
From Left: Symbols from Creation 6 typeface by the author / Cardboard pictogram from Pictogram-me workshop / Symbols used by the US Department of Transport / Runes
Below: Bente Irminger with her new pictogram partner, Pictogram-me

Linguistic Community

The group of people making the agreement became known as a linguistic community. As long as a community remains intact, changes in language are likely to be small and everyone can easily adopt or be aware of the changes in meaning. If the community splits, then the changes will take different directions with different agreements and eventually the members of one community will have difficulty in understanding the other.

This idea of arbitrary representation based on agreement freed art from a tyranny of words and was explored with much invention by visual artists. The paintings by the surrealist artist René Magritte in his series *The Key of Dreams* (1930) show a collection of objects arranged in a grid,

Each one is labeled as in a child's picture book. However, in this case, three of the images are incorrectly labeled while the fourth is labeled correctly. *In The Betrayal of Images* (1929), Magritte labels an image of a pipe with the phrase "This is not a pipe." Both these paintings highlight the arbitrary nature of language and invite the viewer to rediscover the ordinary. This presented the opportunity for artists to make poetic associations between signifiers and the signified. Wittgenstein, a philosopher and contemporary of Magritte's, wrote that

"the aspects of things that are most important for us are hidden because of their simplicity and familiarity." [3]

1.5

1.5
René Margritte:
The Betrayal of
***Images,* 1928-29.**

The text beneath the painting is neither true nor false. It is not the physical reality of a pipe; it is a representation of a pipe, a painting of a pipe, a signifier for "pipe" but not a pipe itself.

1.6
Marcel Broodthaers,
The Farm Animals,
1974.

The viewer attempts to make new signs by searching for associations between the cows and the car manufacturers.

In a later example, the pop artist Marcel Broodthaers uses the same principle to label a series of cows with the names of automobile manufacturers (*The Farm Animals,* 1974). In this case, the viewer makes new signs in their mind's eye by searching for an association between the images taken from nature and the names from international manufacturing.

Charles Sanders Peirce is the philosopher who is recognized as the founder of the American tradition of semiotics. Whereas Saussure was primarily interested in language, Peirce was more interested in how we make sense of the world around us. Peirce's model for the sign is triangular and deals with the sign itself, the user of the sign, and the external reality—the object (O)—referred to by the sign.

In the model on page 23, the sign (sometimes referred to as the representamen S/R) is very similar to Saussure's signifier (Sr). This is the physical evidence of the sign. This can be, for example, a word, a photograph, a painting, or a sound. Saussure's signified (Sd) becomes the interpretant (I) in Peirce's model. This is not merely the user of the sign but a mental concept of the sign, which is based on the user's cultural experience of the sign. The interpretant is not fixed. It does not have a single definable meaning, but its meaning can vary depending on the reader of the sign. The emotional response to the word "book" will vary depending on the reader's experience of books. For some it may be a comforting and affectionate response based on a lifetime of reading and escape through literature, where for others it may be a suspicious and defensive response based on the book as an instrument of official institutions.

ENSEIGNEMENT AGRICOLE   TABLEAU A

LES ANIMAUX DE LA FERME

CHEVROLET — CADILLAC — CHRYSLER — MASERATI — FIAT — JEEP — LAND ROVER — AUSTIN — ROLLS ROYCE — MERCEDES — VOLKSWAGEN — BMW — CITROEN 2 CV — SIMCA — RENAULT 4 L

Nachdruck von Marcel Broodthaers

1.6

Grammatology and Deconstruction

Saussure saw writing as a visual "copy" of speech.
The signifiers involved are a system of signs that "represent"
speech. The philosopher Jacques Derrida challenged this
notion of opposites, in which speech was somehow the
"original" and writing a mere facsimile. In 1967 Derrida
introduced the term "grammatology," which he described as
the study of writing as a form of representation. To support
this new field of inquiry he proposed a new methodology,
a mode of research to investigate grammatology. Derrida
called this new approach "deconstruction." This was a
wider view of how language operated that included a wider
range of non-phonetic elements as part of the system.
Poststructuralism proposed that the artist and the designer
were not masters of a language but operated within a matrix
of possibilities of code and that this code extended beyond
signifiers that represented a sound, the alphabets.

In deconstructing the relationship between speech and
writing, Derrida showed that speech does not represent
reality any more or any better than writing does. Both
speech and writing fail to fully capture reality. Phonetic
writing is more than a secondary translation of speech and
uses a number of signs that are not phonetic in order to
attempt a fuller description of reality. Some of the signs used
in writing come from a range of other sources—numbers,
mathematical symbols—and many do not represent
anything distinct and can be open to interpretation.
Writing includes space, punctuation, flourishes, deletion
marks—all of which have no phonetic value. Deconstruction
is a term that has often been applied to an approach to
typography. This approach would include a study of the
various graphic marks and conventions that are part of the
typographers toolkit—visual marks that are used alongside
or within typographic compositions, as well as the use of
space underlying grid structures.

This references another idea called "Parerga," defined by
Kant as a group of elements that surround a piece of work
yet are part of it—a set of signs that are "about the work" yet
are outside it. A frame, for example, sits outside a piece of
work, such as a painting, but is read as part of the work.

If we return to writing, we can then imagine that space
is not an accessory to the writing but indeed part of that
writing. The same might be true of frames, rules, underlines,
strikethroughs, exclamation marks, and so on. They are
external forces acting on the internal content, yet they are
not neutral and have a distinct effect on the content. They
are connected to the content yet not directly part of it, but
they are part of the whole act of reading the content. Inside
and outside begin to interchange and work to influence each
other; the frame becomes part of the painting.

S d { (Ö) s } I R

S

1.7

1.7
Combined Model
for a Sign.

On the left is
Saussure's model for a
sign and on the right
the version proposed
by Peirce. As we can
see, the two models
are remarkably similar
despite the difference
in terminology.

Charles Peirce

*"A sign is something which stands to
somebody for something in some respect
or capacity. It addresses somebody, that
is, creates in the mind of that person
an equivalent sign, or perhaps a more
developed sign. The sign which it creates
I call the interpretant of the first sign. The
sign stands for something, its object."*[4]

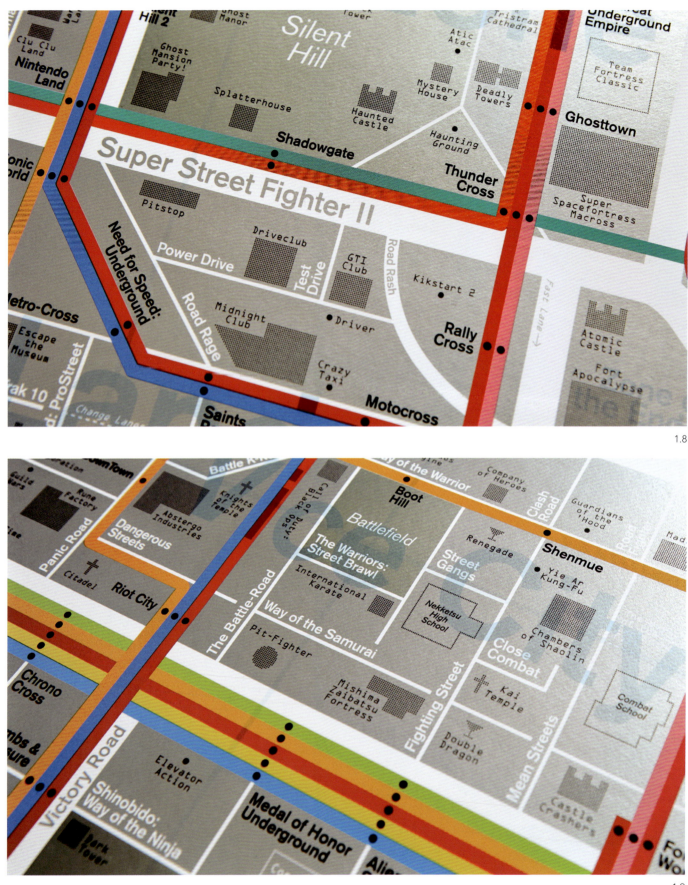

1.8

1.9

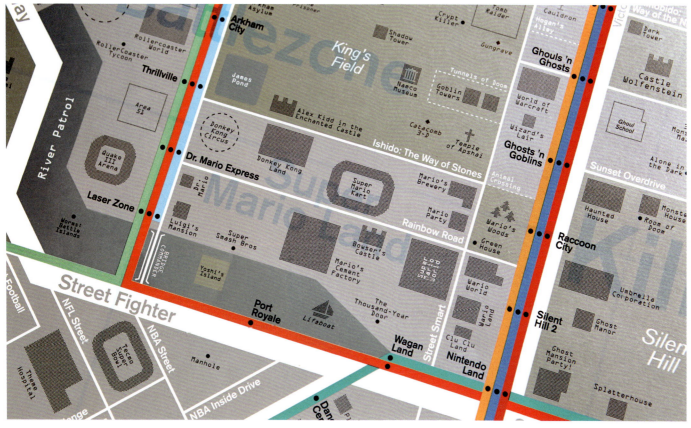

1.10

1.11

1.8–1.11
Creator: Dorothy
Title: Game Map
Exemplifies: Agreement/Linguistic Community

A street map made up of the titles of more than 500 video games and other references from the history of gaming—from the early titles of the 1950s such as *OXO* and *Tennis for Two* to contemporary best sellers like *Grand Theft Auto*, *Call of Duty*, and *Assassin's Creed*.

The imaginary map is loosely based on an area of Tokyo, the city that was home to some of the all-time classic arcade games that paved the way for the modern-day gaming industry. The names of the districts, streets, train stations, and buildings have all been replaced with new names drawn from different genres of gaming such as survival horror (*Silent Hill*, *Resident Evil*, *Sweet Home*), beat-'em-ups (*Street Fighter*, *Streets of Rage*, *Double Dragon*) and Nintendo classics (*Super Mario Kart*, *Donkey Kong Land*, *Luigi's Mansion*).

To a reader not conversant with gaming, the map might be read literally as a real place. The composition of the poster, with its flat blocks of color overlaid with text, is understood as a map, as this is an agreed language we learned

from an early age. In such a context, a series of parallel colored lines punctuated with black dots is read as a public transport network. The reader understands the text as station names or place names because of the familiarity of this context. This is cleverly reinforced by the choice of text and its relationship to the graphic language. What appear to be streets, for example, carry the linguistic signs that one would expect, such as Tiger "Road" or Power "Drive." Similarly, district names have the conventional geographical references we have learned to expect of place names, such as Silent "Hill" and Kings "Field." The poster successfully carries two languages at the same time with the possibility of communicating to more than one linguistic community—the visual language of mapping, which sets the context, and the linguistic language that references gaming. The map carries a series of symbolic and iconic signs (see also "Categories of Signs" in Chapter 2), while the gaming references may depend on our individual experience (see also "Habitus" in Chapter 5).

1.12

1.13

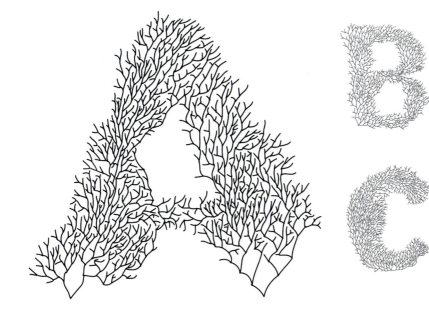

1.14

1.12
Creator: Hansje van Halem
Title: Schrank8-PinarViola
Exemplifies: Agreement/Duality

Screen-printed poster taken from a series designed for self initiated Schrank8 Homegallery, Amsterdam.

1.13
Creator: Hansje van Halem
Title: BlockC-NadineStijns
Exemplifies: Agreement/Duality

Screen-printed poster taken form a series designed for Galerie Block C, Groningen.

These posters show a variety of different representations of a phoneme or sound. The shapes we know as roman letters are well understood and deeply embedded in our visual language, so the author can improvise around these basic shapes to the point of abstraction without losing the basic meaning.
At the foot of the poster, these alphabetic signs are presented in a simpler form and combined with other signs to make words, which in turn are signifiers for places, gallery names, and dates. Clearly, these signs are arbitrary, as the relationship between the sign and the thing it represents is not evident to the reader other than as a learned relationship. This arbitrary nature of signs is known as duality.

1.14
Creator: Hansje van Halem
Title: Branches ABC
Exemplifies: Agreement

A type specimen based on the way that tree branches grow. In this example, the author has taken liberties with the letterforms as each of them becomes a pictorial form. Despite this, they remain readable, as they are very familiar shapes whose meaning has been agreed upon and learned by a linguistic community.

1.15–1.17
Creator: Migrantas
Title: A Visual Language of Migration
Exemplifies: Agreement

Working with public urban spaces as a platform, Migrantas uses pictograms to provide visibility to the thoughts and feelings of people who have left their home country and now live in a new one. The team develop workshops together with migrant women, translate drawings into pictograms, and display them in the urban environment. The signs representing man and woman have been learned as part of a distinct system and form part of an international agreement. These shapes are used as a template to create new signs that describe the issues and feelings of the workshop participants. New elements are added that also carry widely agreed meaning, such as a heart or a globe for example. This enables the messages to be universally understood by a broad audience, as these signs transcend spoken language. In some cases, the imagery is distinct to a particular community—a particular headdress, for example—and the agreement is more locally understood within a smaller linguistic community. In many cases, the signs can be easily understood on their own; however, when there is no agreed sign at hand to describe what they want to communicate, then text is used, which introduces yet another set of signs to the composition (see also "Anchorage and Relay" in Chapter 4). The signs for man and woman are used individually but can also be read as global signifiers—representing not just a single woman or man but a community of women and men (see also "Metaphor and Metonym" in Chapter 2).

Not a terrorist

1.15

1.16

1.17

SIENA CATHEDRAL
EARLY HISTORY

The origins of the first structure are obscure and shrouded in legend. There was a 9th-century church with bishop's palace at the present location. In December 1058 a synod was held in the church resulting in the election of pope Nicholas II and the deposition of the antipope Benedict X.

In 1196 the cathedral masons' guild, the Opera di Santa Maria, was put in charge of the construction of a new cathedral. Work was started with the north – south transept and it was planned to add the main, larger body of the cathedral later, but this enlargement was never accomplished.

By 1215 there were already daily masses said in the new church. There are records from 1226 onwards of the transport of black and white marble, probably for the construction of the façade and the bell tower. The vaults and the transept were constructed in 1259-1260. In 1259 Manuello di Ranieri and his son Parri carved Roman wood choir stalls, which were replaced about 100 years later and have now disappeared. In 1264, Rosso Padellaio was paid for the copper sphere on top of the dome.

A second massive addition of the main body of the cathedral was planned in 1339. It would have more than doubled the size of the structure by means of an entirely new nave and two aisles ranged perpendicular to the axis existing nave and centred on the high altar. The construction was begun under the direction of Giovanni di Agostino, better known as a sculptor. Construction was halted by the Black Death in 1348. Basic errors in the construction were already evident by then, however, and the work was never resumed. The outer walls, remains of the extension, can now be seen to the south of the Duomo. The floor of the uncompleted nave now serves as a parking lot and museum, and, though unfinished, the remains are testament to Sienese power, ambition, and artistic achievement.

Underneath the choir of the Duomo, an earthax containing important late 13th-century frescoes (probably about 1280) was found and excavated in 1999-2003. The frescoes depict scenes from the Old Testament and the life of Christ. This was part of the entrance of an earlier church. But when the baptistry was built, this under-church was filled with rubble. The earthax is now open to the public.

The bell tower has six bells, the oldest one was cast in 1149.

1.18–1.19
Creator: Matt Varker
Title: Sienna Typeface
Exemplifies: Agreement/Duality

A typeface inspired by the decorative architectural features of Sienna Cathedral. Each letter of the Roman alphabet has been assigned a graphic symbol that can be used to replace the letter in a block of text. The relationship between the symbol and the letter of the alphabet is arbitrary, in the same way as the relationship between the letter and the phoneme it represents. Over time, the reader would become familiar with the shapes and be able to read the code as part of a linguistic agreement. The author has arranged the balance of the well-known symbols (the Roman alphabet) and the new symbols (Sienna) in such a way that readers gradually learn the new code as they work through the booklet. In the first chapter, only the letter A is replaced with Sienna, the second chapter has both the letters A and B replaced, and so on until the final page of the publication, which is presented purely in the Sienna code.

1.18

Exercises

Exercise 1: Context

Collect a number of simple set graphic marks that all have the same origin (for example, a set of crosses as featured on p. 15). If you are not sure where to start, you could reference international road or safety symbols. Here you will find marks and images that have a number of meanings depending on their context and the ways they are combined.

Generate or collect a series of contexts or locations. These could be images cut from old magazines or photographs you have taken yourself. Ensure variety in the examples you choose (for example, a variety of periods, locations and compositions).

Using a pin-board or sketchbook, position the marks on the different contexts. Think about how the meaning of the mark shifts depending on the context, its color, its scale or the period in which it is placed. Write some brief notes to accompany each example as you reflect on the compositions. Try to figure out why you read each one in a particular way and where you learned to do so. Keep these in your notebook for future reference.

Exercise 2: Duality

Using well-known symbols that function as a set, create a short narrative without using words. The symbols could be from a child's reading book (see p. 16) or from the US Department of Transport (see p. 19). Think about how you can change the meaning of a symbol by changing its relationship to other symbols. Try changing the scale, placing one symbol inside another, making a symbol from multiples of another symbol or cutting them up and joining them to other sections of other symbols. Choose a familiar narrative so that you can concentrate on how to translate rather than writing a story. You could use a familiar short journey, a regular routine or a classic fairy-tale as your narrative.

Once your narrative is complete, ask a partner to read the story from the pictures. Compare this story to the one you had in mind and use any differences as the starting point for a discussion about why the stories varied.

2. **W. Chafe**, *Meaning and the Structure of Language* (University of Chicago Press, 1970).

3. *Philosophical Investigations* (1953), in S. Gablik, *Magritte* (Thames & Hudson, 1970).

4. **J. Zeman**, "Peirce's Theory of Signs," in *A Perfusion of Signs*, ed. T. Sebeok (Indiana University Press, 1977).

Chapter Two
How Meaning Is Formed

Categories of Signs

This chapter looks at the various ways in which meaning is formed in a sign. Both Saussure and Peirce agreed that in order to understand how we extract meaning from a sign we need to understand the structure of signs.
To help us do this they categorised signs in terms of the relationships within the structures.

"In a language state everything is based on relations" [5]

Peirce defined three categories of signs:

Icon. This resembles the sign. A photograph of someone could be described as an iconic sign in that it physically resembles the thing it represents. It is also possible to have iconic words, where the sound resembles the thing it represents. Onomatopoeic words like "bang" or "woof" could be described as iconic language.

Index. There is a direct link between the sign and the object. In this category, smoke is an index of fire and a tail is an index of a dog. Traffic signs in the street are index signs: they have a direct link to the physical reality of where they are placed, such as at a junction or at the brow of a hill.

Symbol. There is no logical connection between the sign and what it means. These signs rely exclusively on the reader's having learned the connection between the sign and its meaning. The red cross is a symbol that we recognize to mean aid. Flags are symbols that represent territories or organizations. The letters of the alphabet are symbolic signs whose meanings we have learned.

As a linguist, Saussure was not interested in index signs; he was primarily concerned with words. Words are symbolic signs. In the case of onomatopoeic words, they can also be iconic signs. Saussure categorized signs in two ways, which are very similar to the categories used by Peirce:

Iconic. These are the same as Peirce's icons. They resemble the thing they represent.

Arbitrary. These are the same as Peirce's symbols. The relationship between the signifier and the signified is arbitrary. It functions through agreed rules.

2.1a

2.1a–2.1c Signs.

2.1a The red cross and the subsequent words are all symbols. The reader will have had to learn the correct codings of all these signs in order to understand their meanings.

2.1b

2.1b An index/symbol. The danger of fire is linked to the forest through its physical position (the sign is on the edge of the forest) and by the use of an ideogram of a tree.

2.1c This sign for a shopping center in Manchester is signposted using an iconic sign, which depends on local knowledge.

2.1c

35

It is important to recognize that whichever terms you use, the categories are not separate and can function together in sets. For example, let's look at the traffic sign that warns us that we are approaching traffic lights. The mark on the sign that resembles the lights is both an icon and a symbol. Because it physically looks like the thing it represents, it can be said to be iconic. However, it is also a symbol. It is part of a set of signs for which we have an international agreement about their meanings. We have learned what the signs mean. We may even have been tested on their meaning as part of a driving test. The red triangular frame around the sign is a symbol, which we understand as a warning sign. Furthermore, when this traffic sign is placed in the street next to the road junction, it also becomes an index sign. In this case, its meaning is in part formed by where the sign is placed. It is an icon/symbol/index sign.

Peirce also identified three levels or properties for signs, which can be mapped on to his triangular model. He labelled these properties firstness, secondness and thirdness.

Firstness. This is a sense of something. It could be described as a feeling or a mood. To say that you are feeling "blue" could be said to function on this first level.

Secondness. This is the level of fact. It is the physical relation of one thing to another. The traffic sign we discussed earlier functions on this physical level of fact.

Thirdness. You could think of this level as the mental level. It is the level of general rules, which bring the other two together in a relationship. It relates the sign to the object as a convention. The association we have in our minds between the Stars and Stripes and the United States is a mental relationship that relies on a convention.

2.2
Classification of Signs

A series of examples of Firstness, Secondness, and Thirdness as defined by Peirce.

Peirce's work on the classification of signs became increasingly complex as he refined his original propositions. In 1903, he divided the properties into three broad areas and classified them accordingly: qualities (firstness), brute facts (secondness), and laws (thirdness). Each of Peirce's original three elements of signification (representamen, object, and interpretant) can be mapped against these qualities and, in turn, each of these qualities can be found within each of the elements. This generated a complex grid of subclassification, as shown above. Every sign has a representamen (sometimes known as a sign vehicle) and so can be classified as a qualisign, a sinsign, or a legisign. Every sign also has an object and can be classified as an icon, an index, or a symbol; similarly, as every sign has an interpretant, it can be classified as a rheme, a dicent, or an argument. All signs then become classifiable as combinations of each of their three elements. In other words, a sign can be one of the three types of representamen, one of the three types of object, and one of the three types of interpretant.

2.3

	Quality	Brute Fact	Law
1 1st	Qualisign	Sinsign	Legisign
2 2nd	Icon	Index	Symbol
3 3rd	Rheme	Dicent	Argument

2.3
Classification.

In the table, the rows are the categories (firstness, secondness and thirdness) and the columns are aspects of being. The diagram underneath shows how these are mapped onto Peirce's elements of a sign: the representamen (or sign), the object and the interpretant.

2.4
David Shrigley:
Red Card.

The representamen of a red card can be seen as a legisign, as its signifying element is primarily due to a law or convention. As an object, it is a symbol because it utilizes a convention that is learned as an interpretant it is an argument because it enables us to understand the signs as part of a general system of knowledge.

2.4

RED CARD

THE HEINOUS NATURE OF THE OFFENCE YOU HAVE JUST COMMITTED OBLIGES ME TO DISMISS YOU FROM THE FIELD OF PLAY. RETURN TO THE DRESSING ROOM AND WAIT FOR ME THERE.

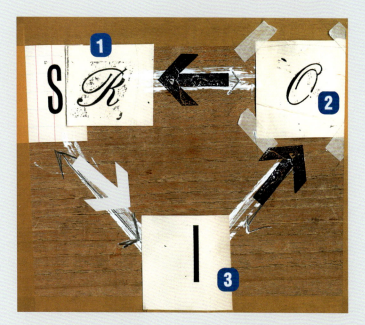

Semiosis

Peirce uses the term "semiosis" to describe the transfer of meaning—the act of signifying. What is distinct about his view of semiosis is that it is not a one-way process with a fixed meaning. It is part of an active process between the sign and the reader of the sign. It is an exchange between the two that involves some negotiation. The meaning of the sign will be affected by the background of the reader; that is, a person's background, education, culture, and experiences will all have a bearing on how the sign is read. One of the most visible examples of this is the symbolic use of color in different cultures. In Western culture, we are familiar with the color black as a symbol of death and mourning. Funeral directors wear black jackets, and it is usual for those who attend to wear black. Athletes wear black armbands to show respect for those who have been lost. This is a symbolic sign that we have all learned and it is also, to a degree, iconic. However, in other cultures across the world this relationship between color and loss is quite different. In China, for example, white is used for funerals, which could create the impression of a wedding to a Westerner, who has quite a different understanding of the symbolic use of white.

Unlimited Semiosis

In the previous chapter, we looked at the terms used by Peirce in his triangular model of a sign. The representamen signifies an object, which in turn conjures up a mental concept, the interpretant, in the mind of the reader. However, when we consider meaning, we must recognize that this triangular process may happen more than once from one starting point. To use Peirce's terms, the interpretant resulting in our mind from the first representamen can then become a further sign and trigger an infinite chain of associations, where the interpretant in one sequence becomes the representamen of the next sequence. This phenomenon, called unlimited semiosis, is commonplace in our reading of signs, and we rush through these chains of meanings at such speed that we hardly notice the chain at all. This is similar to Barthes' structure of myths, which is based on Saussure's model of the sign.

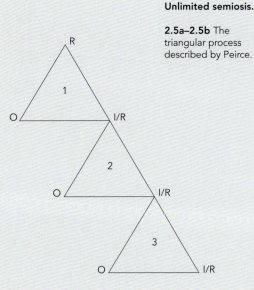

2.5a
Unlimited semiosis.

2.5a–2.5b The triangular process described by Peirce.

2.5b

Value

"Language is a system of interdependent terms in which the value of each term results solely from the simultaneous presence of others."[6]

For Saussure it was what he called "value" that determined the meaning of a sign. Saussure focused on the relationship between the sign and the other signs in the same system. He looked at what we mean by something in relation to what we do *not* mean by something. In his system, book means not magazine, not poster, not film. Saussure has a different term for the transfer of meaning. He calls this "signification." For Saussure, signification is achieved by using the mental concepts—the signifieds—to categorize reality so that we can understand it. The signifieds are artificial things that are made by us and our society and culture.

They are part of our communication system, which is unique to our particular culture. The meaning comes not from the relationship of this sign to reality, which can be arbitrary, but from the relationship between the sign and the other signs around it. To illustrate this, Saussure describes language as a sheet of paper with thought on one side and sound on the other. We cannot cut the front of the sheet without cutting the back at the same time. Sound and thought cannot be divided.

This is essentially a theory of combination and substitution, which Saussure explains using the terms syntagm and paradigm.

If we cut the sheet of paper into three pieces, the meaning of each piece does not come from the relationship between the front and back of the paper but from the relationship of one piece to another.

thought

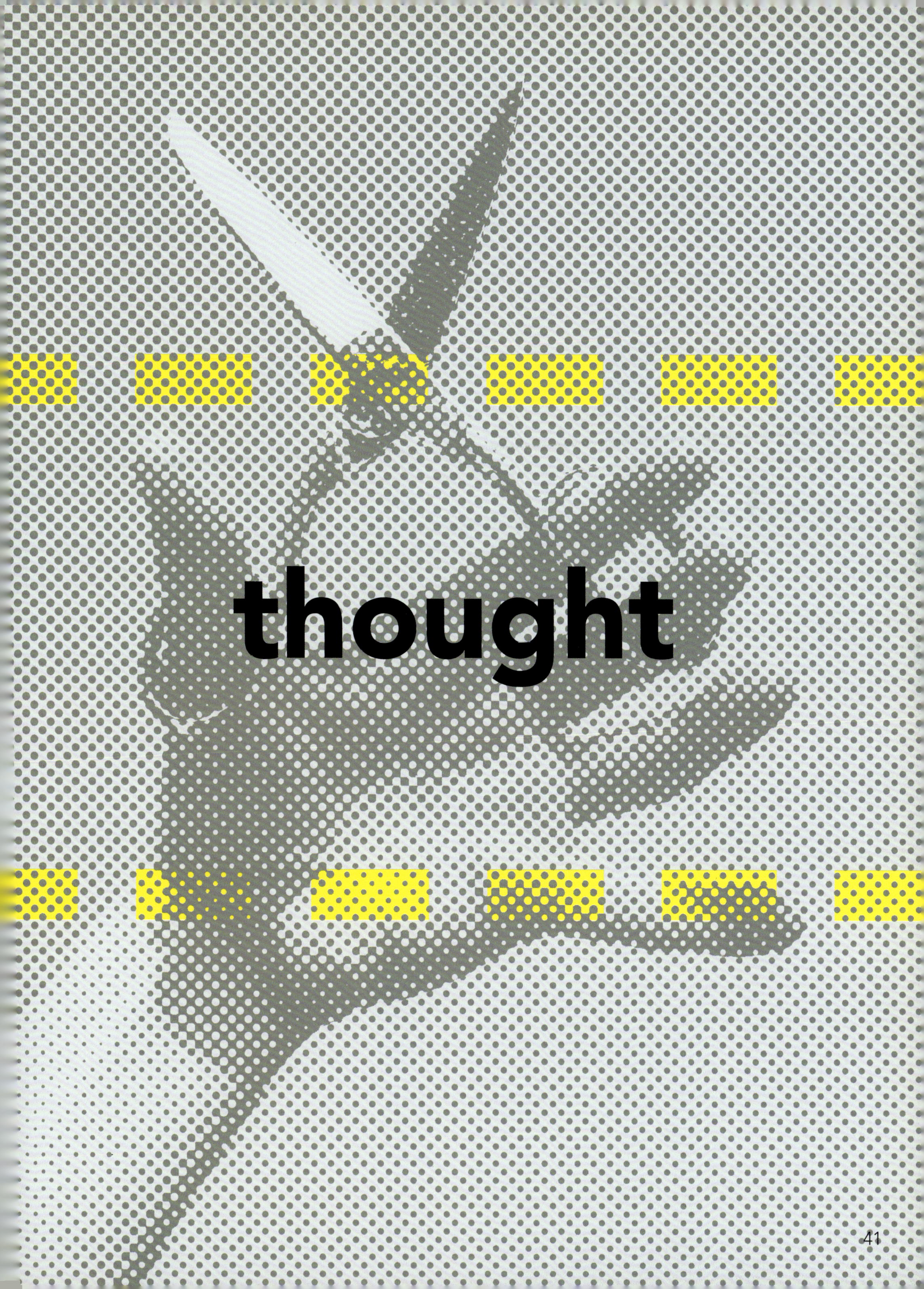

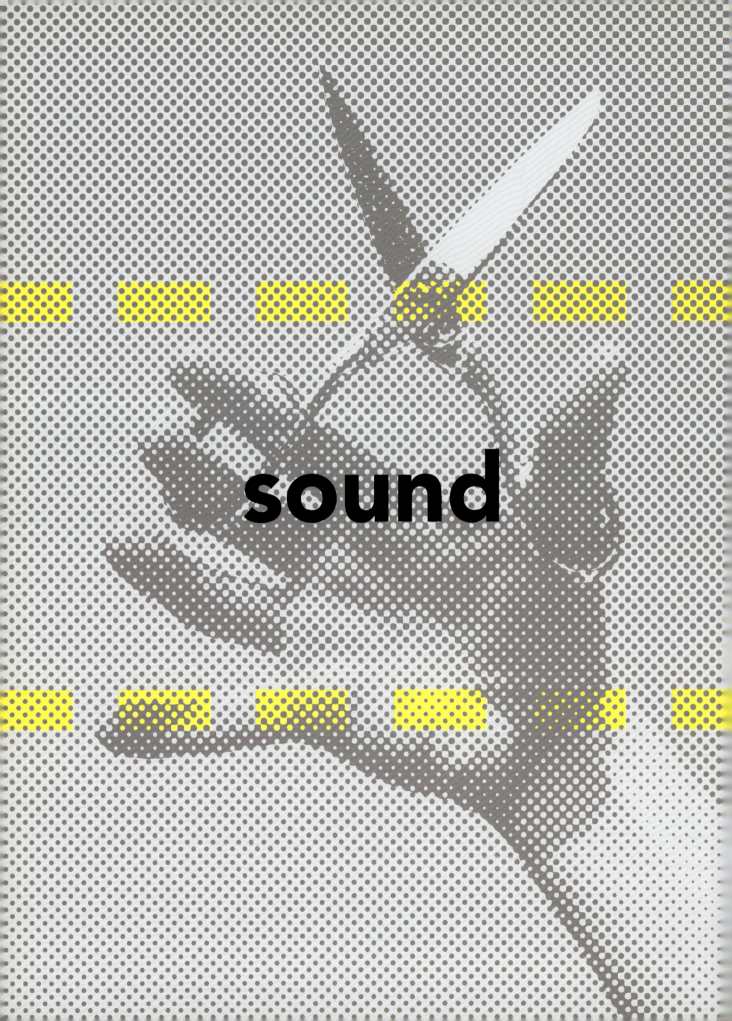

The value is always composed of two things: (1) a dissimilar thing that can be exchanged. (2) a similar thing that can be compared.

Syntagm

This is a collection of signs that are organized in a linear sequence. The word "book" is a syntagm using a set of units: b/o/o/k. A sentence is also a syntagm. Take the sentence "The girl reads the book." The words are the signs, which are arranged into a syntagmic sequence, in which each sign has a syntagmic relation to the signs that go before it and after it. The value of the sign "book" is affected by the other signs around it.

In visual terms, the clothes we wear are a syntagm made up of units, which are the individual garments. The garments themselves are also syntagms, with each garment made of units such as sleeves, collars, and cuffs. As in the previous examples, the value of these units (signs) can be affected by their combination with the other signs. We all create syntagms every day, where the combinations are governed by conventions. These conventions or rules are a feature of the syntagm. When we are writing, we call this convention grammar; when we are dressing ourselves for the day, we might call it taste.

"The idea or phonic substance that a sign contains is of less importance than the other signs that surround it. Proof of this is that the value of a term may be modified without either its meaning or its sound being affected, solely because a neighboring term has been mollified."[7]

Paradigm

The meaning we get from a collection of signs (signification) does not come from these linear combinations alone. When we are making combinations of signs, whether they are words, sentences, or outfits, we are faced with a series of individual choices where we can substitute one sign for another in the same set.

We can take the letters of the alphabet as a simple example. These are all part of a paradigm that we recognize as part of the same set. "A" is part of the paradigm that is the alphabet, whereas "5" is not and "+" is not. When we make choices from this paradigm, we create words that are part of another set of paradigms, such as nouns or verbs. If we substitute an "n" for an "o" from the alphabet paradigm in the syntagm "b-o-o-k" to form "b-o-n-k," we change the meaning entirely. The way that we use language creates another set of paradigms, such as legal jargon, technobabble, and bad language. When writing poetry, we could describe the rhyming words as paradigms based on sound.

In typography, we could say that FF Din Regular is part of a paradigm that includes the entire set of weights that make up the FF Din family; this family of typefaces, in turn, is part of the paradigm of sans serifs. The way we affix one part of a garment to another is a choice made from a set of possibilities that form a tailoring paradigm. The way we choose to apply color to a painting is part of another paradigm. In video, the way we edit from one sequence to another is a choice made from a paradigmical set of conventions in which the "fade," the "dissolve," and the "cut" all have meanings of their own. In music, it may be the way we arrange sounds together to form melody. Our choice of car and the choices we make to decorate our homes with objects are made from sets of paradigms.

Codes

As we can see from these examples, some paradigms, such as the alphabet or the number of weights in a typeface family, have a fixed number of units to choose from. These types of paradigms are made of codes, which are called digital codes. These types of codes are easy to recognize and understand because the units are clearly defined.

Other paradigms do not have a fixed number of choices; the range of choice is unlimited and the divisions between the choices are unclear. The marks produced by a paintbrush or the sounds used in music could be described as paradigms that use codes with no clear distinction between the choices. This type of code is called an analogue code. In practice, it is common for us to attempt to impose digital notation on analogue codes to help us categorize and understand the codes. Musical notation, for example, is an attempt to do just this.

**2.6
David Crow,
Creation 6.**

Sketches from the development work for the Creation 6 font. Each subset within the font is a paradigm in itself. The symbols circled are all part of a paradigm of found images, which in this instance represent various events.

2.6

The two basic characteristics of a paradigm are that:
(1) the units in the set have something in common.
(2) each unit is obviously different from the others in the set.

2.7

2.7
Football Formations and Value.

A combination of seemingly random objects are given meaning by the presence of the goalposts.

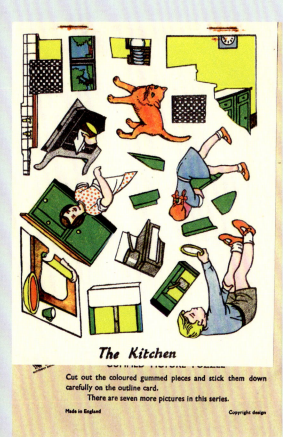

2.8

2.8
The Kitchen.

A set of fragments of imagery from a children's game. The individual pieces are part of a paradigm of images that can be used to assemble a complete picture. The black-and-white drawing gives a guide to the publisher's preferred arrangement.

45

Metaphor and Metonym

Understanding the practical application of paradigmical choice may be easier using the terms metaphor and metonym[8]. When we substitute one word or image in a sequence for another, we can transfer the characteristics of one object to another.

This use of metaphor is very common in advertisements, where a product is imbued with particular properties it is not readily associated with. We can also apply this type of metaphoric substitution to other forms of media. The paradigmical choice to remove the sleeves from a Savile Row pinstripe suit and refasten them using safety pins, would entirely change the way the suit is read.

We would naturally make assumptions about the individual wearing the suit based on this change. The pins are part of a paradigm of fasteners. That they are not normally used as the conventional way of fastening a well-tailored suit can be used to change the meaning of the suit. The irreverence and immediacy of the pins is transferred to the suit and would become part of our overall reading of the garment and the statement that it makes.

A metonym works in a similar way except that it is used to represent a totality. When we want to signify reality in some way, we are forced to choose one piece of that reality to represent it. For example, if we want to represent all children, we might use an image of a child. In this case, the image of one child is being used as a metonym to represent the whole, all children. With all these paradigmical choices, meaning comes largely from the things we did not choose. There is not necessarily any fixed number of options in a paradigm; meanings of words, images, and gestures change over time through the natural evolution of social change. The important thing to remember is that where there is choice, there is meaning.

2.9a–2.9b
David Crow,
Nervous Robot.

2.9a The characteristics of a butterfly in flight are used as a metaphor for feeling nervous by simply placing the image in the stomach of the robot.

2.9b The dark cloud is used as a metaphor for bad news. Placing an image of a political figure inside the cloud associates the bad news with that figure. The value of the sign has been formed by its relationship with the other signs around it.

The important thing to remember is that where there is choice, there is meaning.

2.9a

2.9b

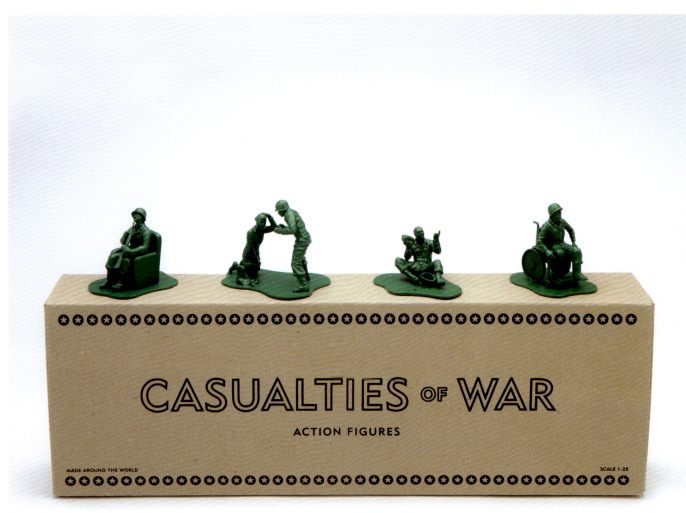

2.10–2.11
Creator: Dorothy
Title: Casualties of War
Exemplifies: Icon/Value

Dorothy designed a set of military figurines to highlight the personal trauma of soldiers returning from war. The set is inspired by a two-part article published in the Colorado Springs *Gazette* titled "Casualties of War." The articles focused on a single battalion whose members, since returning from active duty, had been involved in brawls, beatings, rapes, drunk driving, drug deals, domestic violence, shootings, stabbings, kidnapping, and suicides. The green resin miniature figures are unmistakable as iconic signifiers for toy soldiers that can be found in toy stores all over the world. The potency of the signifier comes from the relationship between the toy soldier and the unexpected gestures and situations in this particular set. What is usually a series of heroic poses of active combat stances is now a series of traumatic personal situations. It is this relationship between these signs that makes the work so powerful. The message the designers intended is communicated through this transfer of value from one sign to the other. As Saussure stated, the value of a sign comes from the other signs around it.

2.11

MARK KOZELEK
SCANDINAVIAN TOUR 2010

Stockholm
Göteborg
Malmö
Oslo
Bergen
Stavanger

2.12

2.13

2.12
Creator: Jason Munn/The Small Stakes
Title: Mark Kozelek – Poster
Exemplifies: Value/Metaphor/Icon

2.13
Creator: Jason Munn/The Small Stakes
Title: Benjamin Gibbard Autumn Tour – Poster
Exemplifies: Value/Metaphor

Both of these posters play with the close connections between music and art. The idea or appearance of a sign is often less important than the other signs around it. We can see in these examples that the value of a sign, a paint pot or a paintbrush, can be modified without changing its appearance but simply by arranging the two signs in a particular way or by adding another sign.
In the Mark Kozelek example, the composition of the two elements is given meaning by the addition of a flat geometric shape that resembles the body of an acoustic guitar. The paint stroke is extended to suggest the neck of the guitar and the streaks of paint are now read as the strings. This relies on compositional geometry that accurately describes an arrangement of elements that is iconic in that it resembles the thing it represents.
The Benjamin Gibbard tour poster communicates purely by bringing the two elements together in a compositional arrangement that we understand as the symbol for a musical note. The paint stirrer is added as a place to site the typography and balances the overall layout, however the meaning does not rely on its being there. The skillful use of color helps to bring the elements together as a single form and draws the reader's attention to the parts of each element that are most important in reading the new symbol.

2.14

2.14
Creator: Jason Munn/The Small Stakes
Title: The Long Winters – Poster
Exemplifies: Metaphor/Icon

In this poster created for Barsuk Records 15th Anniversary shows, the recorded music is literally wrapped up for the winter in a warm scarf. The warmth and comfort of the scarf is metaphorically transferred to the music by superimposing one over the other. Concentric circles arranged in these proportions automatically conjure up the idea of vinyl in an iconic visual representation that looks visually like the object. The grooves of the vinyl are added to help this iconic representation, in this case described by the weave of the scarf.

2.15–2.18
Creator: Sarah Illenberger
Photography: Reinhard Hunger
Title: The Nineth Annual Year in Ideas
Exemplifies: Icon/Index/Metaphor/Semiosis

2.15
Cover Illustration
The thought bubble, commonplace in comic strips, is combined with a collection of illuminated lightbulbs in this photo illustration that brings together the graphic symbol for thought with the classic metaphor for ideas.

2.16
Empty Beer Bottles as Dangerous Weapons
This image was created to accompany forensic research about whether a beer bottle could be considered a dangerous weapon. The photo illustration relies on the iconic shape of a well known weapon and the iconic shape and material of the beer bottle to directly connect the concept of danger to the object.

2.17
Bicycle Highways
To accompany a piece about cycle lanes in Copenhagen, the simple addition of the road markings to a bicycle tire overlays one iconic signifier (the road) with an index sign for cycling (the bicycle tire).

2.18
Thirdhand Smoke
An illustration to accompany a body of work about the dangers of "thirdhand smoke"—compounds left over that settle in the home. The juxtaposition of a a plume of smoke from a baby's soother changes the value of the signs. The use of color also dramatically shifts our usual reading of the soother and the reader connects the second order signifier of the child's mouth with smoke and discoloration which are index signs for ill health.

2.16

2.17

2.18

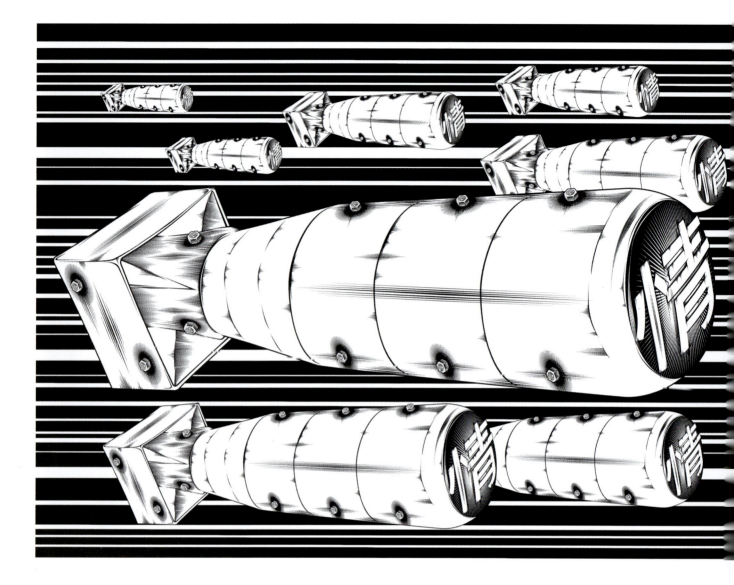

2.19–2.20
Creator: PHUNK
Title: Love vs Love
Exemplifies: Metaphor/Anchorage

In the imaginary Universe of PHUNK, the bomb is used as a universal symbol of power in the linked theme of destruction and creation. The bombs are set on a collision course engraved with the words (Ai) Love and (Quing) Compassion on each bomb. The power and force of the impending explosion is turned into a positive explosion of goodwill as the full force of these bombs is transferred metaphorically to the concept of love and compassion. Applying text to an image is a technique that helps the reader to read the message very clearly and removes any ambiguity in the image (see also "Anchorage and Relay" in Chapter 4).

2.19

2.20

2.21
Creator: Dan Funderburgh
Title: Vigilant Floral
Exemplifies: Value

This wallpaper design is a wayward take on the often "twee" world of surface pattern. It references well-known conventions in the decorative arts that represent a sense of heritage and tradition, and this is what you see at first glance. However, on a closer inspection the reader finds images of surveillance cameras among the foliage that signals contemporary urban anxieties.

The signs that were most obvious are now undermined, as they are juxtaposed with a set of signs from urban social realism, a distinctly different paradigm. The value of the most obvious sign is now affected by the other signs around it, and the reader is invited to compare and contrast an idealized vision of our society with the contemporary social reality of the world around us.

Exercises

Exercise 3: Icon/Index/Symbol

Collect a set of graphic signs from the environment. Categorize these signs as "icon," "index," "symbol," or a combination. Using these signs as a starting point, redesign them so that they fall into a different category. For example, redesign the sign for the shopping center on p. 35 as a symbol rather than an iconic sign. This would mean that the sign was clearly about "shopping" rather than relying on recognition of the center's architecture. Similarly, you could try redesigning signage from your local area based on the architecture rather than on the function or service. This way you will generate an iconic signage system. You could test the results on a sample group of residents, paying attention to whether the system gradually breaks down the further you move away from the area.

Exercise 4: Value

Take a series of photographs that aim to tell a story about a particular issue. You could choose a "big" issue like environmental waste or site your work closer to home with an issue that is important to your local community. Make multiple prints of one or two of the images that you consider most successful at telling the story. Using these images, make a series of cropped versions of each photograph. You are effectively changing the value relationship between a sign and the signs that surround it. How does the meaning change as you edit what is visible in the photograph?

Exercise 5: Relationships and Meaning

Collect a series of photographs of recognizable objects and/or people. Choose images that are unambiguous and iconic. Using these images, make a series of visual sentences in your sketchbook, in which the central or key image is unchanged but the images on either side vary from sentence to sentence. Write down a sentence in words as your eyes read the images and then reflect on whether the key image changed in meaning, despite not being modified in any way. When you feel confident at generating and reading these sentences, then work the other way round. Find three sentences with a common key figure or word and generate the imagery to describe each sentence.

Exercise 6: Metaphor

Using the same series of images as in Exercise 3, look for ways in which two or more of the images can be combined to transfer the properties associated with one image to something else. For example, on p. 47 the idea of being nervous, often described as "butterflies," is transferred by simply placing a butterfly inside the stomach of a robot. Make something feel natural or clean or dangerous, for example, by finding images that can be used to generate a metaphor when combined with something else.

5. F. de Saussure, *Course in General Linguistics* (Fontana, 1974; 1st ed. 1915).

6. F. de Saussure, *Course in General Linguistics*.

7. F. de Saussure, *Course in General Linguistics*.

8. R. Jakobson and M. Halle, *Fundamentals of Language* (Mouton, 1956).

Chapter Three
Reading the Sign

The Reader

The meaning of any sign is affected by who is reading that sign. Peirce recognized a creative process of exchange between the sign and the reader.

Although we can see many similarities between Peirce's interpretant and Saussure's signified, it is clear that Saussure wasn't concerned with the relationship between the signified and the reality to which it refers. The reality that Peirce calls the object does not feature at all in Saussure's model. Saussure was concerned only with language, and he did not discuss the part played by the reader. His theories concentrated instead on the complex structures of language that we use to construct words and sentences:

> "A science that studies the life of signs within society is conceivable; it would be a part of social psychology and consequently of general psychology; I shall call it semiology (from the Greek 'semeion' sign). Semiology would show what constitutes signs, what laws govern them. Since the science does not yet exist, no one can say what it would be; but it has a right to existence, a place staked out in advance. Linguistics is only a part of the general science of semiology; the laws discovered by semiology will be applicable to linguistics, and the latter will circumscribe a well-defined area within the mass of anthropological facts." [9]

However, the meaning of words can change depending on who reads them. In the United States, Peirce had created a theory that saw the reading of signs as part of a creative process.

3.1

Barthes

In Europe, it was Roland Barthes, a follower of Saussure, who took the theoretical debate forward. In the 1960s, Barthes developed Saussure's ideas to consider the part played by readers in the exchange between themselves and the content. For Barthes, semiotics takes in much more than the construction of words and their representations; it takes in any system of signs, whatever the content or limits of the system. Images, sounds, gestures, and objects are all part of systems that have semiotic meanings. Barthes described complex associations of signs that form entertainment, ritual, and social conventions. These may not normally be described as language systems, but they are certainly systems of signification. Whereas Saussure saw linguistics as forming one part of semiotics, Barthes turned this idea upside down and suggested that semiotics, the science of signs, was in fact one part of linguistics. He saw semiotics as "the part covering the great signifying unities of discourse." [10]

Barthes pointed out that there was a significant role to be played by the reader in the process of reading meaning. To do this, he applied linguistic concepts to other visual media that carry meaning. Like Saussure and Peirce before him, Barthes identified structural relationships in the components of a sign. His ideas center on two different levels of signification: denotation and connotation.

Whereas Saussure saw linguistics as forming one part of semiotics, Barthes turned this idea upside down and suggested that semiotics, the science of signs, was in fact one part of linguistics.

3.2

3.1
Iceberg.

3.2
Boy.

A black-and-white photograph can be read as nostalgic. A negative could be a reference to the process of photography or to forensics and crime. A close-up draws our attention to the emotional aspect of the subject; the coarse dot reproduction suggests low-quality printing and can in turn suggest either newspaper journalism or political campaigns.

Denotation and Connotation

This first order of signification is straightforward. It refers to the physical reality of the object that is signified. In other words, a photograph of a child represents a child. No matter who photographs the child and how the child is photographed, in this first order of signification, the image still just represent "child." Even with a range of very different photographs, the meanings are identical at the denotative level. In reality, we know that the use of different film, lighting, or framing changes the way in which we read the image of the child. A grainy black-and-white or sepia-toned image of a child could well bring with it ideas of nostalgia; a soft focus might add sentiment to the reading of the image; a close-up crop of the face could encourage us to concentrate on the emotions experienced by the child.

All these differences are happening on the second level of signification, which Barthes called connotation. The reader is playing a part in this process by applying knowledge of the systematic coding of the image. In doing this, the meaning is affected by the background of the viewer. As in Peirce's model, this humanizes the entire process. Connotation is arbitrary, in that the meanings brought to the image are based on rules or conventions that the reader has learned. The consistent use of soft focus, for example, in film and advertising has found its way into our consciousness to the degree that it is universally read as sentimental. Because conventions vary from one culture to another, it follows that the connotative effect of the conventions—the rules on how to read these images—will also vary between communities.

Convention and Motivation

Convention is an agreement about how we should respond to a sign. We have already mentioned conventions such as the close-up and the black-and-white image. Conventions such as these pepper the images we read today. We instinctively know that slow-motion footage does not mean that the action is happening slowly. We understand that we are supposed to use this as a signal to study the skill of the action or admire its beauty. The roughly rendered typography of the rubber stamp indicates a gestural immediacy. It suggests the informal. We can almost hear the sound that the stamp would make when the image was made. So much of meaning comes from convention that signs with little convention need to be very iconic in order to communicate to a wide audience. Another way of describing this is to say that a sign with little convention needs to be highly motivated.

Motivation is used to denote how much the signifier describes the signified. For example, a photograph is a highly motivated sign because it describes in detail the subject in the image. It looks like the thing or the person it represents.

Using the term provided by Saussure and Peirce, it is iconic. A highly motivated sign is a very iconic one. Using the complementary terms, an arbitrary sign (Saussure), or a symbolic sign (Peirce), could be described as unmotivated. Using the earlier example, a photograph of a child is highly motivated, while a cartoon image of a child is less motivated. In the photographic example, the arbitrary element is confined to the framing, focus, and so on, whereas with a cartoon the illustrator has more freedom to take liberties with the reality of how the child actually looks. However, the less a sign is motivated, the more important it is that the reader has learned the conventions that help to decode the image.

3.3–3.6
Nous Vous, Green Man Figures.

Opposite and overleaf: These illustrations created for the Green Man festival are based around six wild and primal "deities," each representing and reflecting a different aspect or area of the festival. Visitors would find them inhabiting their lush and bountiful surroundings on the Green Man website, around the festival site itself, and on all printed material and merchandise.

They demonstrate how an author can take liberties within representation. Here the illustrators distort the relative sizes and shapes of physical anatomy in highly unmotivated signs. The audience, however, has no problem decoding these because the images draw from a well-understood convention.

3.3

3.4

3.5

3.6

Language and Speech

We could think of the differences between the first and second order of signification as the differences between what we say and the way we say it. Saussure distinguished between the two, which he called "langue" and "parole." However, as we have seen, Saussure's primary concern was the system—the language, or "la langue." Language, says Barthes, is language minus speech[11] yet at the same time it is a social institution and a system of values. Speech, according to Barthes, is an individual act of selection and actualization. Barthes introduces the distinction between systems of language and speech by providing examples. In what he calls the garment system, Barthes describes language as the parts of a garment, with the rules of language governing the association of parts. Speech in the garment system would then be the individual way of wearing the garment, the personal quirks, the degree of cleanliness, size, the free association of pieces, and so on. In the car system, the variations in the way we drive would make up the plane of speech. This correlates closely with Willis' ideas of symbolic creativity[12], which relate exactly to these types of everyday expression. Thus, we can say that when people adopt different hairstyles, for example, although they are using the same language (the hairstyle system perhaps), they are using different forms of speech—speaking differently or, to use the terminology of French sociologist Pierre Bourdieu[13], using different dialects. Using the example of the rubber stamp, the words are the language, and the qualities of the stamp are the speech. The idea of using tone of voice is useful to those who use typography as a communication tool.

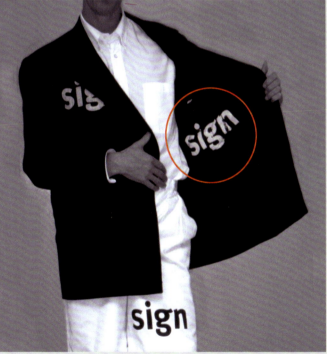

Myth

Barthes sought a new approach to semiotics that would force us to look more closely at what we take for granted in our visual culture. In his essays on myths in contemporary culture[14], Barthes drew attention to a range of misconceptions in French society about the properties and meanings we attach to images of the things around us—the purity of washing powder, the sport of wrestling, the Frenchness of wine. Barthes was angered by the way contemporary society confused history with nature. For him, myths were the result of meaning generated by the groups in society who have control of the language and the media. These meanings are seen as part of the natural order of things. Where these meanings came from and the process that transformed the meaning of the signs are either forgotten or hidden. The process of generating myths filters the political content out of signification. In today's society, modern myths are built around such things as notions of masculinity and femininity; the signs of success and failure; what signifies good health and what does not.

In today's society, modern myths are built around such things as notions of masculinity and femininity; the signs of success and failure; what signifies good health and what does not.

**3.7
Seel Garside,
Ladies Night.**

Angelina, Buffy, Catherine, Demi, Elizabeth, Fiona, Gwyneth, Helena, Isabella, Julia, Katie, Laura, Mia, Nicole, Olivia, Patricia, Queenie, Rachel, Sandra, Theresa, Uma, Victoria, Winona, Xena, Yoko, Zoe.

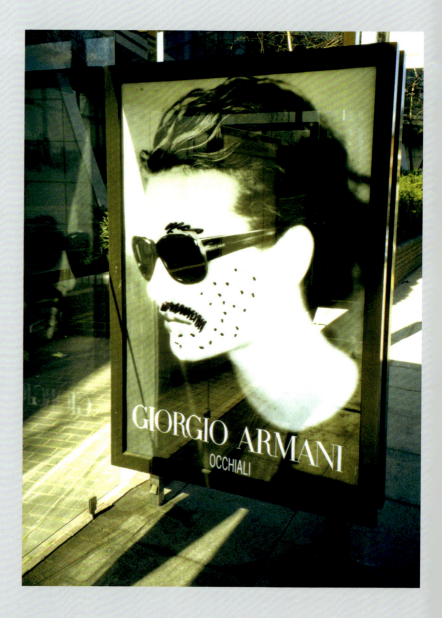

3.7

3.8–3.9
Art Direction: Sagmeister and Walsh
Design: Santiago Carrasquilla, Wade Jeffree
Photography: Henry Hargreaves
Title: Adobe 24 Hours
Exemplifies: Language/Speech

Adobe approached Sagmeister and Walsh
to interpret their MAX typography and their
Creative Cloud logo. Using basic materials in an
empty studio, the designers created a playful
representation as a creative performance that was
streamed live on a Times Square billboard. The
central motifs are well known and form part of a
language of marks associated with the client. The
versions created in the 24-hour session change
the speech by giving the logotypes a distinctly
new tone of voice.

3.9

3.10
Art Direction: Stefan Sagmeister, Jessica Walsh
Design: Stefan Sagmeister, Jessica Walsh,
Santiago Carrasquilla
Photography: Henry Leutwyler
Creative Retoucher: Erik Johansson
Title: SVA – Take it On
Exemplifies: Language/Speech

A series of posters created for the School of
Visual Arts (SVA) in New York City. The design
team recreated the message by introducing
three distinct versions of the text, with three
different voices, described by applying unique
personalized lettering to each of their faces.
The maxim "Take it On" could be described as
the language in these compositions, while each
version brings its own speech.

3.10

3.11–3.13
Creator: Jon McNaught
Title: Pilgrims
Exemplifies: Connotation

Jon McNaught creates silent narratives capturing quiet moments of everyday life as miniature sequential comic strips, in this case a visit to a remote cathedral. The narrative of the visit with a guided audio tour runs in parallel with the story of Adam and Eve from the Garden of Eden. A number of conventions are employed to help the viewer understand the overall narrative. The use of light for example, helps us separate the religious narrative on the stained glass from the story of the visit itself. The washed out backlit figures clearly differentiate themselves from the "live" action with high contrast light and shade created by a single light source. As viewers we understand the convention of an individual being spot lit through a stained glass window as a moment of religious symbolism. Our attention is drawn to the lone figure reading a book on the front bench as a shaft of light passes through the main illuminated panel of the "original sin." In another frame the forbidden use of a camera is clearly signaled as a white flash of light before the offender is chastised. As readers we expect comic strips to carry dialogue as text panels. Other conventions being used in Pilgrims include the omission of text that renders the story silent and adds an eerie atmosphere to the visit. The high number of frames devoted to very small moments like removing a pack of gum from a handbag, slow the story down in a similar way to a slow motion film sequence. At the end of the story the author introduces a folded price tag that is universally understood as he draws attention to the commodification of religion and the figurine souvenir is slipped into the handbag alongside the gum we saw earlier in the story.

3.12

3.13

3.14

3.15

3.16

3.17

3.14–3.17
Creator: Typeworkshop–Underware
Title: Manual Pixelism
Exemplifies: Language/Speech

A workshop held by Underware at Ecole cantonale d'art de Lausanne, Switzerland. Participants were asked to search for an interesting shape that worked well as a repeated module for a "pixel font." The "Dream On!" Group used grocery carts to render the letters (*the language*) in an unconventional form. This unconventional speech conveys a sense of scale and drama along with a gritty urban realism in the supermarket car park. The "Read On" Group connected publishing to the idea of "freedom" simply by rendering, or speaking, the words in an unusual way.

3.18

3.18
Creator: Joe Magee
Title: Belieber – Guardian Newspaper
Exemplifies: Denotation/Connotation

A complex image commissioned in the wake of the arrest of Canadian teen pop singer Justin Bieber in Miami, Florida, on a drunk driving charge after he was caught drag racing in a sports car on a main thoroughfare. The resulting media outcry about his failing as a role model to his 48 million teenage "Beliebers" was rubbished by the writer, Marina Hyde, who asserted that, although he has passed into a realm of cult leader or even deity, children have always idolized personalities from popular culture, and parents should not be so quick to take the moral high ground.

The source material is Beiber's police mug shots. These images exist in the first order of signification, denotation, as a straightforward representation of the subject. By duplicating the profile shot, the author creates a triptych, creating the connotation of a religious portrait. This connoted reading is then emphasized by the addition of a starburst graphic—a convention signifying a deity in religious painting. The final overlay of graphic lines and circles suggests social media networks and literally obscures the real person underneath.

3.19
Creator: Joe Magee
Title: Sochi, 2014 – Time Magazine
Exemplifies: Symbol/Language/Speech/Metaphor

A *Time* cover commissioned to illustrate how the upcoming Russian Winter Olympics in Sochi had become a high security operation with the Olympic area surrounded by an unprecedented circle of fences, roadblocks, and security checks because of the threat of terrorism.

The cover emulates a classic Olympic poster featuring an idealized sporting figure in action alongside the universally known symbol for the games. In this version, the Olympic rings are formed from barbed wire, changing the way the symbol is spoken to something much more sinister. The wire logo could also be described as a metaphor, as the anxieties of high security are literally transferred to the symbol (see also "Metaphor and Metonym" in Chapter 2).

3.19

3.20
Creator: Joe Magee
Title: Tebow – Time
Magazine
Exemplifies:
Connotation/Speech.

This image
accompanied an
article about American
footballer Tim Tebow,
who became renowned
for overt on-field
displays of his Christian
faith. "Tebowing"
became a new verb
in the United States—
kneeling on one knee
with head bowed and
an arm resting on the
one bent knee. The
image is a rendition
of the sportsman
within the context
of a stained glass
window in the act of
"Tebowing." By itself,
the act of kneeling in
this way is a relatively
open sign and might
not be read as a
religious act. However,
when this gesture
is represented as a
stained glass window,
the reader brings the
context and the act
together and is left in
no doubt. Religious
connotations are clear
because the gesture is
"spoken" in a religious
manner.

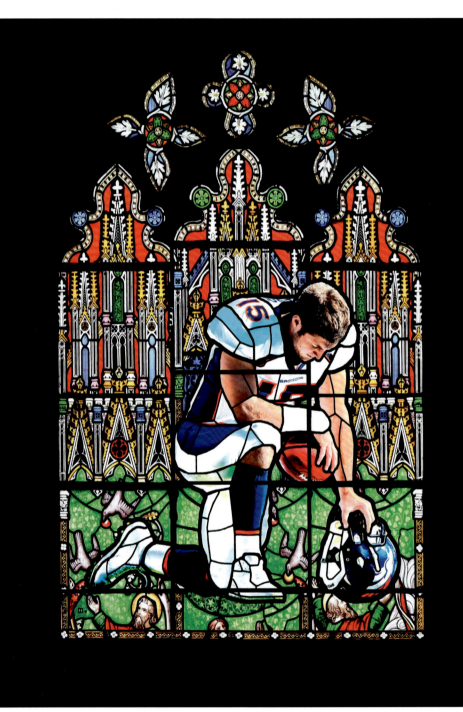

Exercises

Exercise 7: Language and Speech

Look through historic examples of signs and symbols, and try to find instances where the meanings have changed entirely—for example, a coat of arms used as a football (soccer) club's crest or university logo. Try drawing these signs in a variety of different ways, using different line qualities. Can you update these original signs by drawing them in a particular way? In other words, can you add contemporary speech to an ancient language or sign? This process could also be reversed. Find a contemporary symbol (perhaps something from a computer interface), and use a medium associated with heritage to see if you can place it in a bygone age.

Exercise 8: Connotation/Index/Metonym

Choose a number of adjectives at random (dirty, beautiful, eccentric, special). Create a roll of tape that features one of these words as a repeat. (In practice, this can simply be a roll of paper made by joining laser printouts together.) Choose a number of exterior or interior spaces that you feel represent your adjectival choices. Mark the space by using the tape you have created in the same way a police force might mark a crime scene. Think about the way the words are displayed (the speech) and the colors you use, and try to find unusual locations where you can use the tape to draw attention to a quality that is not immediately obvious. Take photographs of the taped spaces. You are playing with various connotations by the way you photograph the locations, but you are also anchoring the meaning of the space by using the words on the tape. The resulting image could be described as an index sign because of the relationship between the word and the location.

9. de Saussure, *Course in General Linguistics.*

10. R. Barthes, *Elements of Semiology* (Cape, 1967).

11. Barthes, *Elements of Semiology.*

12. P. Willis, *Common Culture* (Open University Press, 1990).

13. P. Bourdieu, *Language and Symbolic Power* (Polity Press, 1991).

14. R. Barthes, *Mythologies* (Paladin, 1972).

Chapter Four
Text and Image

Digital and Analogue Codes

For linguists, codes must be digital—that is, they are composed of a fixed number of digits or units. In *Image, Music, Text*, Roland Barthes[15] asks whether it is possible to have codes that are analogical.

Digital codes are paradigms in which all of the units in the set are clearly different from each other. (As we saw in Chapter 2, the two basic characteristics of a paradigm are that the units in the set have something in common and that each unit is obviously different from the others in the set.) The alphabet is arguably the most common example of a digital code.

Analogue codes are paradigms in which the distinctions between units are not clear; they operate on something more like a continuous scale. Music or dance, for example, could be described as analogue codes. However, many analogue codes are reduced to digital codes as a means of reproducing them in another form. Musical notation, for example, reduces the analogue qualities of sound to distinct notes with individual marks.

4.1
Jas Bhachu Rubik's Cube Font Generator.

Each individual part of the drawings that we recognize as letterforms is separated out in an ingenious "Rubik's Cube" of geometry that can be combined to make any letter of the Roman alphabet. The geometric shapes form a digital code.

4.2
Vintage stencils.

Where the "digital" code is contained as a paradigm on brass strips.

4.2

Advertising Writing

To examine the relationship between text and image, Barthes chose to focus on compositions from advertising. In advertising, the reader can be sure that signification is always intentional. Nothing is left to chance. It is the purpose of the advertisement to communicate the positive qualities of the product as clearly as possible to the chosen audience. This is demonstrated by Frank Jefkins' three basic principles of effective advertisement writing:

1. The advertisement should be of interest and value to the reader. The writer should ask himself, "How can I interest my prospects in my proposition? How can my offer be of service to prospects?"

2. The advertisement should be precise, that is, get to the point as quickly as possible; hence the success of the most hard-worked word in advertising, FREE!

3. The advertisement should be concise, saying what it has to say in the fewest necessary words, remembering that an encyclopedia of many volumes can be concise compared with a verbose novel.[16]

4.3

4.4

The Three Messages

**4.3
Paul Davis, Wasteland.**

The text answers the question "What is it?" Our attitude to the humble cracker is fixed by the addition of a copy line in a parody of advertising.

**4.4
Alan Murphy,
Watership Down.**

The charming drawing of the rabbit is changed by the addition of the text. Without the text we would have no idea what story was causing the rabbit so much anxiety. The text on the book cover anchors the content of the book for us. The text in the "bubble" also gives us an insight into what the rabbit is thinking and how it might express itself. This is a relay text, as it gives us information that we would not get from the drawing and advances the narrative.

Barthes sets out a system for reading text/image combinations, which comprises three separate messages. The first message is described as the linguistic message. This is the text itself, usually in the form of a slogan or a caption to the image. Reading the linguistic message requires a previous knowledge of the particular language employed. The linguistic message can also carry a second-order signifier by implication. For example, an advertisement featuring the word "Volkswagen" tells us the name of the manufacturer but also signifies certain national characteristics. Notions of high design standards and precision engineering are read at the same time as the name.

The second message is the coded iconic message. This is a symbolic message and works on the level of connotation. The reader is playing a part in the reading by applying knowledge of the systematic coding of the image. An image of a bowl of fruit, for example, might imply still life, freshness, or market stalls.

The third message is described as the non-coded iconic message. A photograph, for instance, could be described as a message without a code. One simply reads the medium as itself: it is a photograph. This works on the level of denotation. Although the linguistic message can be easily separated from the other two messages, Barthes maintains that the other two cannot be separated because the viewer reads them at the same time. In other words, the medium cannot be separated from the message—a phenomenon Marshall McLuhan pointed to in his book *The Medium Is the Massage*.[17]

Anchorage and Relay

Text on an image, according to Barthes, constitutes what he calls a parasitic message, designed to quicken the reading with additional signifieds. The addition of text can be a powerful method of altering or fixing the meaning of an image. This is something that is present in a great number of the images we read—in captions, subtitles, film dialogue, and comic strips. However, it seems that neither the length of the linguistic message (the text) nor its position is particularly important, but merely the presence of the linguistic message itself. Indeed, it is possible that a long text may comprise only one message, a single global signified. When coupled with an image, text has two possible functions: anchorage and relay.

Anchorage, says Barthes, directs the beholder through a number of possible readings of an image, through what he calls a floating chain of signifiers, which causes the reader to ignore some of the signifiers and read others. The text answers the question "What is it?" Text on a connoted image (the coded iconic message) helps the reader to interpret the signifiers being presented. Text on a denoted image (the non-coded iconic message) aids recognition. Barthes describes the way in which the reader is directed by remote control to a meaning that has been chosen in advance. He points out that this often has an ideological purpose. Anchorage text can thus have a repressive value when applied to an image.

The second possible function, relay, is much less common. The text is usually a snippet of dialogue and works in a way that is complementary to the image. It can be found in comic strips, for instance, and is particularly important in film. Relay text advances the reading of the images by supplying meanings that are not to be found in the images themselves, as in film dialogue.

4.5

4.5
Pineapple.

A combination where you expect the text to fix the meaning, but it creates confusion instead.

"What is it?"

Roland Barthes

4.6

4.7

4.8

4.6–4.8
Creator: Stephen Appleby
Title: Guide to Life, from the Loomus Series for The Guardian
Exemplifies: Anchorage/Relay

A selection of drawings from the wonderfully esoteric world of Stephen Appleby. Stephen frequently uses relay text in his work. In the treadmill image that shows the cycle of life, the story is relayed to us via text, using phrases like "First Step" and "First Day at School."

The text also describes mechanical sounds and includes direct speech to help the reader get the full narrative. In the instructional cartoon the diagrammatical notations are anchored by the additional text and the smile of the cat's face is confirmed by the text above.

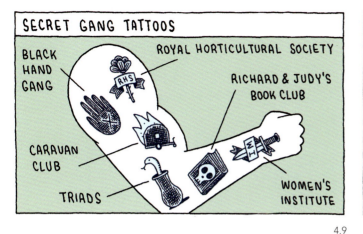

4.9

4.10

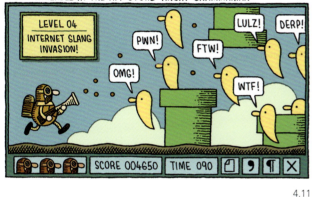

4.11

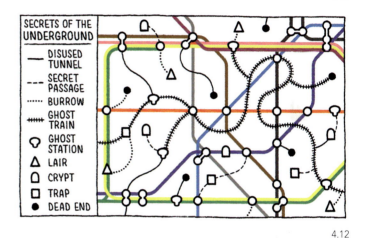

4.12

4.9
Creator: Tom Gauld
Title: Secret Gang Tattoos
Exemplifies: Anchorage

A set of tattoos is explained by the addition of text. Most of the signs have elements that we might recognize. Some have initials we might be familiar with and many of them have some images that are characteristic of tattoos—text banners, the sword and the skull, for example. These conventions help us understand the images as tattoos rather than just drawings. However, at face value they are very open signs and it is necessary to *anchor* the meaning by adding text.
The sign captioned "Richard and Judy's Book Club" for example, showing a book adorned with a skull, could have a number of other meanings were it not for the text. This would depend on what personal experience the reader brought to the image. However with the text added, the reader is directed to a single reading from the range of possibilities. It is this relationship between what we might bring to the meaning juxtaposed with what the text says that gives the cartoon its humor. In this example the signifier carried by the text will only communicate to a particular community, as "Richard and Judy" are a middle-aged married couple who present together on daytime TV in the United Kingdom.

4.10
Creator: Tom Gauld
Title: Elderly People
Exemplifies: Anchorage

This set of road signs proposes a set of variants based on a single conventional safety sign warning drivers that elderly people are likely to be crossing the road (slowly). In this set, a number of additions have been made to the original symbol that draw on visual conventions from different paradigms. "Elderly Revolutionaries," for example, references the flag-waving imagery common to images of political rallies and revolutionary political posters.

4.11
Creator: Tom Gauld
Title: Angry Grammarian
Exemplifies: Anchorage/Relay

In this imaginary platform game, the text works in two different ways. The text above and below the drawing anchors the context of the frame as belonging to a game, with its reference to the app store, levels, and a scoring system. The other text, however, functions as relay text and replaces the sound of the game, carrying the narrative and explaining what is happening in the scene beyond what the reader can get from the visuals alone. If this were a game with the sound on mute, the player would not know why the main character was trying to eliminate the "tweets."

4.12
Creator: Tom Gauld
Title: Secrets of the Underground
Exemplifies: Anchorage

A set of geometric symbols that are commonly used to mark a place or a route are given a sinister meaning on the map legend as their meaning is anchored by the addition of text. The slightly ambiguous symbol used to describe the "Ghost Station" makes much more sense when we read what it stands for.

4.13

13 June 10.45pm woman with dog.

11 October 8.05pm. Clockwork tin Cat.

4.14

4.15

22 october 8.05pm. Two ceramic dogs and a tin one.

4.16

26 April 7.02pm. Fat Freddie asleep on his cushion

4.13–4.17
Creator: John Hewitt
Title: Daily Drawing Series
Exemplifies: Anchorage/Relay

These works, produced one a day, are drawn from events, objects, and ideas that arise in the daily life of the author. Almost all of the several hundred drawings have some form of text alongside them. In many cases, the text will anchor the image either geographically or in time. The drawings are often made quickly and have an economy of mark-making that makes it difficult to communicate some details. In other cases, the text will explain something that couldn't be discerned without being present. The drawing made on February 8 at 6:05 p.m., for example (4.13), gives us some relay text that tells us Teddy (the dog) is lying on the cushion because he is "feeling unwell." In other cases, such as the drawing of three dog figurines (4.15), we can only guess from the drawings what the dogs are made of; the anchorage text explains their material to the viewer as "two ceramic dogs and one tin one."

4.17

91

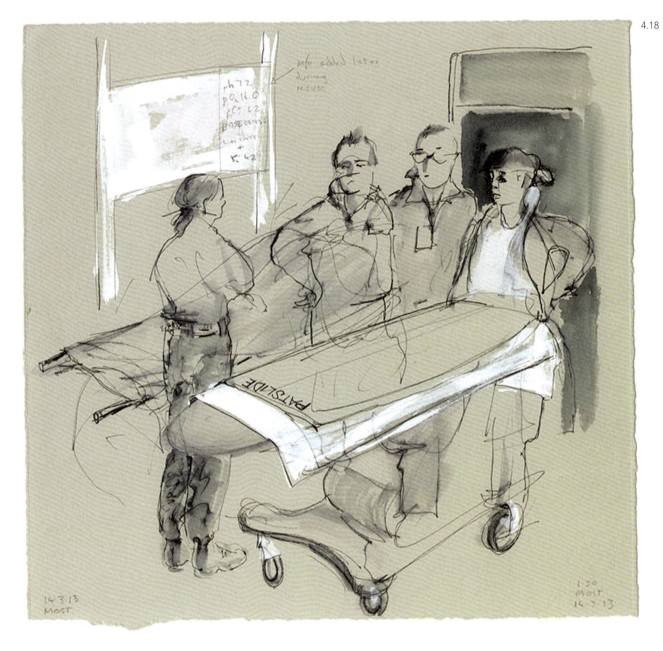

4.18–4.21
Creator: Julia Midgley
Title: War, Art & Surgery
Exemplifies: Anchorage/Relay

These works, produced for an illustrated book and an exhibition, chart the training of military medics before their deployment to Afghanistan and the recovery of wounded soldiers on their road to recovery. As documents, they are edited by their author in the very making of the work and communicate a particular interpretation of the events. To a documentary illustrator, annotating the drawings with text can serve a number of functions. As the original drawings are often made in difficult situations and with limited time, they are annotated to help the illustrator when reworking the drawings back at the studio. For example, Julia has worked with patients undergoing strenuous rehabilitation and physiotherapy, drawn surgeons training, and worked inside helicopters and on training exercises in a Hercules aircraft. The finished drawing will then carry text that helps the viewer to understand a wider range of detail beyond what can be immediately understood. This can be factual contextual detail like the date and time of events, or it can be a clue to what was happening or what was being said at the time.

4.20

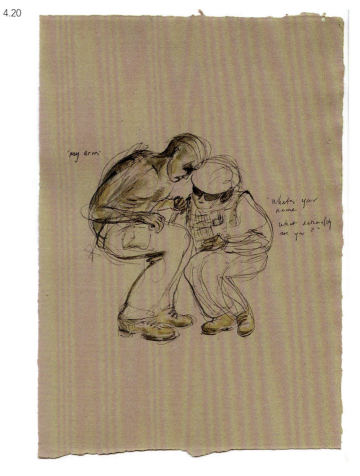

4.21

4.22

4.22 Creator: Paul Davis
Title: Ceci n'est pas un Logo
Exemplifies: Anchorage/Connotation

The text in this drawing anchors the work as a reference to conceptual art of the early twentieth century. The example draws directly from *The Betrayal of Images* (1929) by René Magritte, featured in Chapter 1. In Magritte's painting, the reader is exposed to the idea that language itself is arbitrary, and the reliability of language is undermined. The connotation in this drawing is the intellectual and theoretical position of the original work, which in this new version undermines the certainty and strength of the corporate brand featured.

4.23
Creator: Paul Davis
Title: DebutArt
Exemplifies: Anchorage/Connotation

In this drawing, the central figure appears to be engulfed in a cloud of thought and confusion. The text above the figure anchors the reason for this confusion as it references the philosophical proposition "I think, therefore I am" made by René Descartes in the seventeenth century. This proposition became a fundamental element of Western philosophy; it proposed that thinking about our existence in itself proves our existence. The self-reflective maxim is given a twist in this version where the readers are invited to participate by bringing their own general knowledge to the work. The connotation of Descartes encourages us to share in the confusion of human existence, apparently lost in an endless and uncertain landscape.

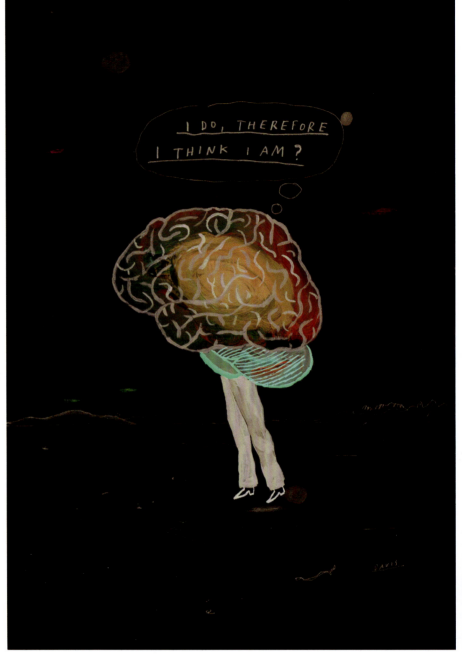

4.23

Exercises

Exercise 9: Duets

Find a photographic image from a magazine or newspaper that you find particularly compelling. Using this image as the starting point, generate an image yourself to accompany your "found" image. Write down all the possible meanings that could be read from having these two images side by side. Overlay a word on one of the images to fix or anchor the meaning of the composition. Try a number of different words to see how this third sign controls the way we read the semiotic relationships.

Exercise 10: Tribes

Find a pictogram that represents either man or woman (see p. 19). Make multiple copies of the pictogram and then add in text beneath each one a different musical style (Rock and Roll, Psychedelic, Indie, Goth). Now amend the pictogram in a way that helps the viewer to better understand the relationship between the image and the text that anchors it.

Exercise 11: Maps

Find ten images that can be reproduced in a small size on a plain background. These could be figures, buildings, objects, or abstract shapes. Make a number of copies of each and arrange them across a surface like a map. Now make a list of the objects like a key below the map and label the images. Repeat this process and think about how the meaning of the map can be entirely changed by the way you label the images on the key.

15. **R. Barthes**, *Image, Music, Text* (Fontana, 1977).

16. **F. Jefkins**, *Advertisement Writing* (MacDonald & Evans Ltd, 1976).

17. **M. McLuhan and Q. Fiore**, *The Medium Is the Massage: An Inventory of Effects* (Allen Lane the Penguin Press, 1967).

Chapter Five
Official and Unofficial Language

Habitus

Pierre Bourdieu classified human endeavor and knowledge in terms of fields. Some fields are clearly defined by making entry into that field difficult to attain; in general, the more difficult the entry, the more defined the field. The field of law might be considered a clearly defined field. Those in the field could be said to be sharing or struggling with a common pursuit and sharing in its own particular discourse. The visual arts would be described as an activity that takes place within the field of cultural production. Like all other fields, this field is constantly changing, as are its membership and its discourse.

The notion of creative and intellectual fields was extended to establish the idea that each field preexists its membership. In the case of the field of cultural production, the field preexists the artist. Within the field are a number of official positions, such as graphic designer, that offer a range of possibilities. These possibilities are limited by a number of factors, such as education, social background, gender, and age. These factors influence choices while also reinforcing the validity of the field. It is generally agreed that individuals carry with them, perhaps subconsciously, some idea of which position to take up on their arrival within the field. You could call this a sense of vocation. It is this sense of vocation that Bourdieu described as habitus. According to Bourdieu, the choice between the territories where we will take up positions as individuals (the choice of habitus within the language) is accomplished without consciousness in every situation[18]. Apparently insignificant aspects of everyday life, such as ways of doing things or body language, and the constructed images we witness every day all contribute to the formation of habitus.

The Production of Legitimate Language

Bourdieu begins his assertions about legitimate language with Saussure's observation that neither languages nor dialects have natural limits[19]. All that is necessary is a set of speaking subjects who are willing to make themselves the bearers of the language or dialect using an intrinsic and autonomous logic. Bloomfield describes this as a "linguistic community—a group of people who use the same system of linguistic signs."[20] Bourdieu, however, goes on to point out that external as well as internal factors affect the limits of a language, and that externally there is a political process that unifies the speaking subjects and leads them to accept, in practice, the use of the official language. In order to successfully impose this language as the official language, it is necessary to have a general codification that is sustained by creating institutional conditions that enable it to be recognized throughout the whole jurisdiction of a certain political authority. It follows that this official language has territorial limits. An unofficial language—a dialect, for example—has not undergone this institutional process of control; it is internally driven by its own independent logic. We will look at this in more detail later in this chapter.

The official language imposes itself as the only legitimate language within a territorial limit. In the context of this book, the territory could be described as the field of cultural production and would include various positions within it, such as graphic designer or artist. This is particularly true of situations that characterize themselves as official.

Grammarians and teachers working from institutions become jurists who examine the usage of language to the point of the legal sanction of academic qualifications. These qualifications identify the legitimate language within a territory and enable individuals to take up positions within a field. If we look at the vocational art and design disciplines of graphic or fashion design, in most cases entry into the field is attained through the successful completion of an academic qualification, such as a degree or a diploma. The process of completing the course generates a portfolio, which is used in selection at interview, but in most cases the interview is only possible once the award has been attained. The use of language, both written and visual, has been judged and sanctioned by an institution:

"The educational system, whose scale of operations grew in extent and intensity throughout the nineteenth century, no doubt directly helped to devalue popular modes of expression, dismissing them as 'slang' and 'gibberish' (as can be seen from teachers' marginal comments on essays) and to impose recognition of the legitimate language."[21]

the
page
itself
is a
sign

The book of Genesis tells the story of the Tower of Babel. At that time, all the citizens spoke the same language and everyone could understand each other. To celebrate this, they decided to build a tower that reached towards the heavens. God in his wisdom decided that this must be stopped; the most effective way of doing this was to fragment their language so that hierarchies would develop. Of course, linguists do not take the story to be an accurate historical text, but it serves as a useful metaphor of how language can be used as an instrument of control.

Shifts in bilingual education in the United States illustrate this well. In an article titled "Language Wars,"[22] René Galindo pointed to a number of propositions passed in the late 1990s. A California English Only initiative (Proposition 63) was followed by a provision for citizens and anyone doing business in the state to sue local governments for actions that diminish or ignore the role of English as the common language of California.

Proposition 227, called English for the Children, was passed in 1998. It decreed that all children be taught English; anyone who wanted their children to be taught a second language would have to make a special written request. Galindo summarized the debate in terms of the

"competition for value between different constituencies that takes place through the manipulation of symbolic assets such as language(s)." [23]

This competition for value can also be seen in the way slang is included in dictionaries as recognized deviations from legitimate language. Slang phrases often appear in italics, a typographic signal of difference or separation, as popular or common uses. Indeed, any value or capital (cultural or monetary) awarded to individuals always arises from a deviation from the most common usage. Commonplace usage is seen as trivial or vulgar. Capital, such as qualifications, is awarded to well-chosen words/signs/ images that are seen as dignified or lofty. As the educational system is funded by and answerable to the state, it could be said that the production of a legitimate language is bound up with the field of economic production.

"Obligatory on official occasions and in official places (schools, public administrations, political institutions etc.), this state language becomes the theoretical norm against which all linguistic practices are objectively measured." [24]

It is worth noting that the highest proportion of graffiti attacks (an extreme form of unofficial visual language) take place in schools, the institutions responsible for the maintenance of the official language, and on local authority (state) property. Bourdieu points out that for a particular language, or a particular use of language, to impose itself as legitimate, the different dialects—whether class, regional, or ethnic group—have to be practically measured against the legitimate language. Without support from external agencies, these dialects or unofficial languages (which are internally driven) cannot be imposed as the norm for another territory, despite the possibility of using these differences as a pretext for declaring one superior to another. The theory follows that these differences can be developed into a system for determining hierarchical position. If we look, for example, at the appearance of the visual language of the pop artists in the 1960s, and the criticism that now accompanies this work, we can see the way in which the discourse surrounding it has developed to authorize the work and enable its acceptance as part of the official visual culture.

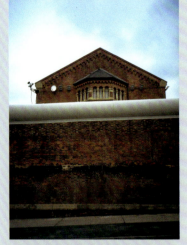

Capital

In its open celebration of popular culture, pop art caused a great deal of consternation among those at the center of the field of cultural production.

> *"There was a widely held view in some circles in the 1950s that serious painting had to be abstract, that it was retrograde for artists to make reference to the outside world by engaging in representation or illusion."* [25]

The British artist Peter Phillips was studying at the Royal College of Art in London, the most prestigious art school in the United Kingdom, marked by its Royal Charter. When he first produced what is now considered some of the finest examples of British pop art, he was castigated by his tutors. Their disapproval was so strong that Phillips was forced to transfer from the Painting School to the less noble, but popular, Television School for his final year. The celebrated David Hockney was threatened with expulsion at around the same time for his refusal to complete (official) written work. Allen Jones fared less well and was expelled from his college. Compare this attitude towards the work with these excerpts from a recent critique on the same work:

> *"Phillips painted a large canvas, Purple Flag, in which he synthesised his practical skills and his intuitive response to Italian pre-Renaissance painting with an open expression of his enjoyment of funfairs and the game of pinball. . . . The smaller motifs incorporated in the lower half of the painting . . . establish an alternative timescale as in early Italian altar pieces, in which predella panels establish a narrative complement to the starkly formal central image."* [26]

This method of referencing the past is commonplace in artistic criticism and appears to lend authority to the work by aligning its formal features with those that are already accepted as part of the official discourse.

> *"Some of the recurring characteristics of pop . . . were anticipated in a variety of developments in European and American Modernism. The basing of images on existing popular sources, for example, had precedents in the work of nineteenth-century painters such as Gustav Courbet and Edouard Manet."* [27]

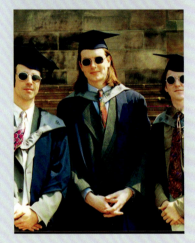

5.1
Capital

Society awards capital to individuals for their use of language. This can be monetary or cultural capital. In the case of good use of the official language, an educational award such as an honors degree or a PhD could be the cultural capital leading to monetary rewards. The reverse is also true for the use of an unofficial language, such as graffiti or vandalism, where a spell in detention could be the reward.

Rules

Visual arts publications, which deal with the craft of making visual work, invariably carry sets of rules on how to successfully employ the official visual language within their various disciplines. Of course, many of these accepted conventions are grounded in experience and are valid observations. The important thing to recognize in the context of this chapter is that there are rules that have become accepted as legitimate practice and are used in education and elsewhere as the norm against which deviation is measured. Here are some examples from graphic design texts:

"the efficiently designed trademark must be a thing of the barest essentials." [28]

"useless elaboration that has been traditionally a feature of bad trademark design." [29]

"typefaces can unquestionably be assessed on the basis of artistic quality irrespective of their fashion status; and, conversely, no amount of fashionable success can change this assessment for better or worse." [30]

"Visual analogies which most clearly illustrate meaning or the spirit of a word should be sought; for example, the letter O could be the visual equivalent of the sun, a wheel, an eye." [31]

Any value or capital (cultural or monetary) awarded to individuals always arises from a deviation from the most common usage. Commonplace usage is seen as trivial or vulgar.

The Competition for Cultural Legitimacy

It is generally agreed that the social uses of language owe their social value to their being organized into systems of differences. To speak is to adopt a style that already exists and is marked by its position in a hierarchy of styles, which corresponds to a hierarchy of social groups. In a sense, then, these different styles/dialects are both classified and classifying by marking those who use them.

Foucault[32] points out that the biological distinction of gender has been overlaid with a systematic set of discourses that have become an organizing principle in recruiting labor and consuming and producing goods—all of which lead to gender-dominated practices.

Bourdieu[33] outlines a competition in which the public is seen as both the prize and the arbitrator—one in which competitors cannot be identified with the competition for commercial success. This is certainly true of the experiences of designers within the field of cultural production, where work that can be identified as commercial is subject to varying degrees of derision. This is perhaps even more intense in the fine arts, where there is reluctance to acknowledge that art is a commercial activity. This declared refusal to meet popular demand could encourage art for art's sake and increase the intensity of emotions between members of an artistic community. Mutual admiration societies appear, which are inevitably accompanied by formal award ceremonies as a result of artists' addressing an ideal reader.

Major and Minor Language

Deleuze[34] explored the relationship between identity and difference. Difference is traditionally seen as a derivative of identity. This view focuses on where X is different from Y and assumes that X and Y are consistent in their character. Deleuze, however, maintains that this idea is flawed because identities are all effects of difference. In other words, identity does not preexist difference but is a product of difference.

When we apply this idea to language, we can see that this changes our perception of what we might call minor languages or dialects based on major (or official) language. Take Black English, for example, a dialect that has its own internal rules and its own grammar. If we want to study that grammar, then we have to apply the same rules of grammar that we would use to study Standard English. Despite the politics and imperialism of language, in purely linguistic terms, Deleuze would say that the idea of major and minor languages is irrelevant.

Minor languages or dialects exist only in relation to the major language. The constants in language are not in opposition to the variables of the dialect; the constants are the result of drawing what is uniform out of the variables. In this way, the major or official language also changes over time as the language is extended and adopts new words and ideas.

Gilles Deleuze

Michel Foucault

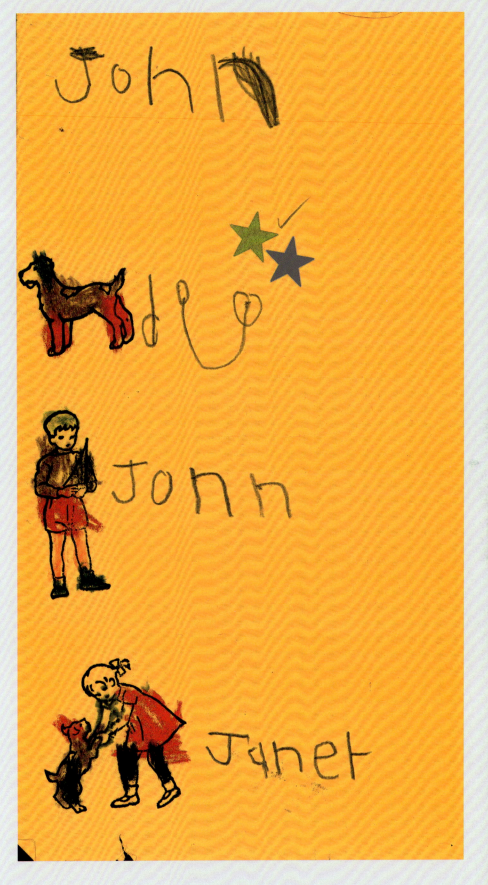

Authorized Language

It is obvious that social conditions and social ritual have a bearing on the use of language. It is a principle of drama that the nature of acts must be consistent with the nature of the surroundings. This phenomenon can certainly be observed within the institutions, mentioned earlier, whose role it is to impose, defend, and sanction legitimate language. The lecture theatre provides an excellent example of Burke's observations on drama. The theatre, the lectern, the books are all instruments of an official discourse deemed worthy of publication. The lecture is granted as legitimate, not by being understood, but by being delivered by an authorized and licensed (qualified) person in a legitimate situation. One notion that is particularly good at highlighting this is what Bourdieu calls "the magical act." This is described as the attempt, within the sphere of social action, to act through words beyond the limits of delegated authority.

The visual arts are full of examples of the magical act, in which the semiotics of the official and the corporate have been skillfully employed to communicate the ideas and feelings of the individual.

> "Suppose, for example, I see a vessel on the stocks, walk up and smash the bottle hung at the stem, proclaim 'I name this ship the Mr Stalin' and for good measure kick away the chocks: but the trouble is, I was not the person chosen to name it." [35]

Being able to recognize and employ legitimate language does not necessarily empower the speaker or artist without another set of conditions. The words themselves have no power unless the user is "authorized" to use them.

ACHTUNG!
PLAKATIEREN
VERBOTEN!
JEDE UNAUTORISIERTE NUTZUNG IST RECHTSWIDRIG UND VERPFLICHTET ZUR ZAHLUNG EINES WERBENUTZUNGSENTGELTS GEM. § 812 BGB UND ZUR ZAHLUNG VON SCHADENERSATZ GEM. § 823 BGB UND WIRD GRUNDSÄTZLICH STRAFRECHTLICH GEM. § 363 STGB VERFOLGT. AUFTRAGGEBER HAFTEN FÜR IHRE ERFÜLLUNGSGEHILFEN.

Unofficial Language

All of us face the problem of a differential fit between how we see ourselves and how others see us. When we try to solve this problem individually, it can lead to isolation, but solving the problem collectively offers us a new perspective on the situation.

Unofficial Codes

Mike Brake[36] points out that the differential fit problem is redefined according to the rules and conventions of the subcultural group and offers us a new identity outside of the usual categories of age, class, or occupation. Young people in particular feel marginalized by official cultural values. They often place no importance on work, even as a means of earning money, and turn instead to leisure-based rather than work-based activities. Increasingly their aspirations are focused on what they do outside of the workplace. Their energies are directed towards activities associated with music, fashion, and sport. Often two or more of these are fused together in a semiotic package.

The football terraces, for example, are lively and colorful places, densely packed with fans adorned in team colors. On one level this merely signifies the team they support. However, studies involving the behavior of football (soccer) fans show that there are a number of subtle messages being communicated. The way the colors are worn, how the scarf is tied, the gestures made by the fans, and the way they dress are all part of a semiotic code. Studies have shown that it is possible to predict which fans would stand and fight, which fans regularly attend away matches, and which fans see themselves as tough but probably aren't—all by looking at semiotic subtleties.

The gestures between rival soccer fans work as metonyms. The clenched fist and the frosty stare are both recognizable as metonyms for real violence and can replace real violence in ritualized aggression. As we have seen previously, Saussure observed that neither languages nor dialects have natural limits. All that is needed is a set of speaking subjects who are willing to make themselves the bearers of the language or dialect. The symbolic gestures discussed in this chapter can be seen as dialects. A whole range of semiotic symbols mark the distinct linguistic communities. What they wear, how they talk, their gestures, and their haircuts are all part of their particular dialect. The language, whether spoken or visual, is determined by the community of people who use it; unlike the official language, it has no control imposed from the outside. It is easy to see why it is an attractive option for anyone who feels, in some way, marginalized by official culture: the opportunity to communicate with like-minded people in a way that cannot be understood by those they mistrust. By its very use, the language also marks the user as part of an alternative community.

Visual Dialect

Let's look, for example, at graffiti as a visual dialect that also carries its own linguistic terms. Graffiti is a useful model because, first of all, it is distinctly visual. It also has the benefit of being an extreme type of unofficial language. It stands well outside of any educational system. This makes it easy to recognize and produces equally clear reactions from those who read it.

"Writing graffiti is about the most honest way you can be an artist. It takes no money to do it, you don't need an education to understand it and there's no admission fee."[37]

One formal feature that is common to most graffiti is the materials used to make the work. The nature of the act dictates that the marks have to be made quickly with materials that can be easily carried and concealed and that are readily available. In addition to scratching, the most popular materials are spray paint and, more recently, the marker pen, which can be customized to give a desired effect (chiseled or taped together). It is worth noting that posting flyers is never mentioned as a form of graffiti and, as Castleman observed, the transport police do not target sticker campaigns. Whether this is due to the permanent nature of graffiti tools or the fact that many commercial or political campaigns use print-based (official) media remains unclear. What is clear is that flyer posting also has many of the features of graffiti:

"Flyposters have provided a cultural form which those on the fringes of, or totally outside dominant cultures, have been able to use with great effect. The uses have varied from person to person and from situation to situation. The common characteristic is that flyposters are a medium for groups or individuals with little money or access to the established media. They are exciting, dangerous and subversive."[38]

Stencil graffiti carries a similar set of semiotic values. As Tristan Manco points out in his book on stenciling, the medium is readily associated with the stencil lettering to be found on functional packaging and urban street furniture. This gives the stencil an authority and an authenticity with the added benefit of consistency. As with the flyposter, our awareness of their history makes stencils exciting and subversive:

"All graffiti is low-level dissent but stencils have an extra history. They've been used to start revolutions and to stop wars. They look political just through the style." [39]

The possibilities of loading messages with these second-order signifiers (danger, subversion, dissent, authenticity, politics) has certainly not been lost on manufacturers and advertisers. The unofficial visual language of graffiti and its associated forms has been used to promote fashion labels, music, cars, clubs, sportswear, foodstuffs, drinks, and events. Whenever a brand wants to communicate directly with a young audience, it can adopt a dialect that suits its particular needs. As well as speaking with the right tone of voice,

unofficial visual language is usually inexpensive to produce, adding to its authenticity. In truth, many of these fail to deliver true authenticity because the context plays such a large part in reading the message. A graphic mark on a cereal box is unlikely to be dangerous and exciting simply because it is on a cereal box.

In art and design, the use of the vernacular is a popular way of adding a layer of perceived authenticity and honesty to a whole range of work. It is often seen as a signal that the marketing department has not been involved in the promotion of a product or service. The vernacular is broadly seen as work that is deliberately undesigned. This draws from a range of visual communication made by amateurs, giving it an informal and unofficial flavor. The work is often made by hand or by using instant design systems such as plastic peg letters.

5.2

5.3

5.2–5.3
Creator: PHUNK
Title: PHUNK Logos
Exemplifies: Official Language

These logos make use of some of the conventions we understand as representing official organizations. The outstretched eagle, the lightning strikes, and the row of stars can be found on military insignia and on the stationery of government departments in many countries. The crossed swords can be found on a range of emblems from religious marks to export/import and military badges. The symmetrical layout and uppercase serif typography also signal official symbols.

5.4

5.5

5.6

5.7

5.4–5.7
Creator: PHUNK
Title: From the Bottom of My Pencil Case
Exemplifies: Official Language

PHUNK explores the theme of "school" in an installation at Singapore Art Museum. The piece features a reconstructed half-life-sized classroom complete with all the visual signals of *official language*—the teacher's desk and chalkboard, miniature desks and chairs for the pupils, and educational graphics on the walls. This sensory work creates an emotional response from visitors by placing them in a part of their childhood that was characterized by the visual theater of legitimate and authorized culture.

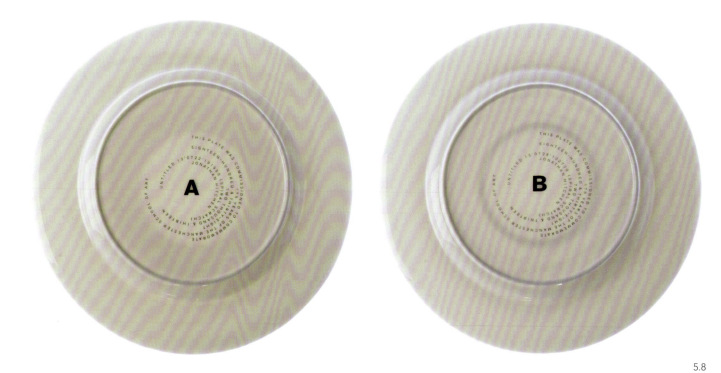

5.8

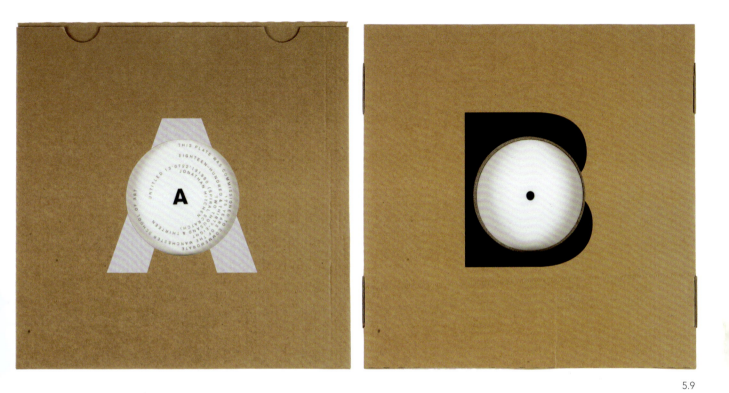

5.9

5.10

5.8–5.10
Creator: Jonathan Hitchen
Title: Commemorative Ceramic Plates
Exemplifies: Authorized Language

Two plates designed to commemorate the
175th anniversary of Manchester School of Art.
The project draws directly on the established
English tradition of producing ceramics to mark
special occasions. These events are usually of
a formal public nature, like a royal wedding,
a coronation, or an official anniversary of an
establishment body. In this version, the author
uses the authorized materials for such a project,
reminding the recipient of the heritage of the
school, but also references the more recent legacy
of popular music connected with the school.
The design draws on another established and
authorized format for music publishing, with the
ceramics becoming a double album of vinyl. The
"spiral scratch" on the top surface is a reference
to a seminal Manchester record, which in turn
references the grooves of the vinyl. This particular
design was generated using a bespoke piece of
code that randomly generates spiral drawings.

5.11

5.11–5.12
Graphic Design: Nous Vous
Three Dimensional Design: Studio Weave
Title: Ecology of Colour
Exemplifies: Unofficial Language

This timber-clad structure in Dartford's Central Park is an outdoor classroom, dyeing workshop, art studio, bird-watching hide, tree house, and park shelter all rolled into one. The exterior pattern was produced as part of a workshop with volunteers who hand-stained the timber panels before assembly. The project embraces the informal vernacular (unofficial) language of the handmade garden shed, found in countless back gardens across the United Kingdom. These spaces are often highly personalized and are often constructed from leftover offcuts of wood with little regard for aesthetics.

5.12

5.13

5.13–5.15
Art Direction: Michael O'Shaughnesy/Uniform
**Photography: Students from Liverpool School
of Art and Design**
Title: Everyman Theatre
Exemplifies: Official/Unofficial Language

Temporary hoardings around building sites are
often the site for corporate messaging which,
because of its public nature, then become a
surface for local personal unofficial interventions
like fly posters and graffiti. In this instance, the
hoardings blur the line between official and
unofficial language by creating a set of highly
personal visual moments that are curated to
embody the spirit of the theatre. The large
hoardings that surrounded the new Everyman
Theatre in Liverpool feature texts and images
that celebrate the city, its creativity, and its
young people. The photographs show a series
of highly personal and inconspicuous fragments
of the city and its people that together create
narratives defining the city. The informality of the
photography is combined with equally informal
handwriting and layout that feels like a large
notebook.

5.14

5.15

5.16
Creator: Jimmy Turrell
Title: nbvnbvnvbnbv
Exemplifies: Official/Unofficial Language

This image contains signifiers that could be described as both unofficial and official in their sources, yet the overall semiotic is of an unofficial piece of communication because of the way the elements have been brought together. The underlying portrait is very formal, with its symmetrical composition, and the lighting and background suggest it has been taken with care in a photographic studio. The jewelry, dress, and hairstyle all suggest a posed portrait, something that belongs to an official way of recording a likeness. However, the misregistered color circles and badly aligned row of typography look as though they have been hurriedly made using the type of low-quality mechanical print process associated with very low budget unofficial underground publishing. The typography relates to official communications, both in its form as a document header and in its content, but its position and misregistered color undermine this and suggest that the source is a found image not authored by the author of the poster.

5.17
Creator: Jimmy Turrell
Title: No Place to Hide
Exemplifies: Unofficial Language/Convention

A piece about Edward Snowden, the computer analyst whistle-blower who leaked top secret NSA documents leading to revelations about U.S. surveillance of phone and internet communications. The unofficial and unsanctioned nature of the act is reflected in a poster that utilizes unofficial visual signifiers. The low-quality photocopied reproduction with its imperfections suggests that the work is produced in unofficial environments and reminds the reader of homemade graphics and underground political activism. The use of the aircraft and the censored text as the Stars and Stripes reminds us how well established this flag is as a symbolic convention.

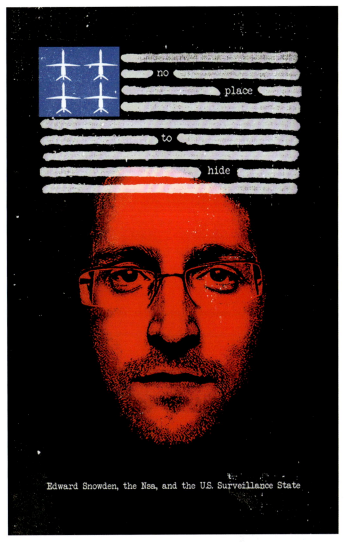

5.17

5.18

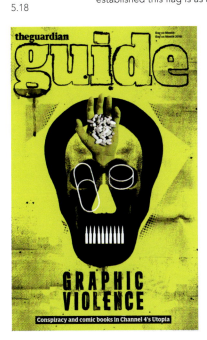

5.18
Creator: Jimmy Turrell
Title: Graphic Violence – The Guardian
Exemplifies: Unofficial Language

The drugs, bullets, and a skull are a semiotic combination that suggest crime and, by association, violence. However, it is the visual language of the illustration that reaffirms the aggression of the title. The low-quality photocopied reproduction, handmade lettering, and random marks that look like unedited mistakes place the reader in an uncomfortable and unsettling environment. The runs of ink in the image remind us of wounds, and the bright yellow and black color combination is a well-understood convention for danger signs.

5.19

5.19
Creator: Katy Dawkins
Title: Interference (Plaque)
Exemplifies: Authorized Language/Magical Act

From a series of graphic interventions in public
spaces. The original text is taken from the
unofficial communication of graffiti, found in
various parts of the city; it is then redrawn using
a legitimate and authorized visual language
before being returned to its original environment.
By using characteristics and materials from an
authorized visual code, the designer is able to
transfer the message from unofficial to official
language. This transfer, acting beyond the
realm of delegated authority, is described as a
magical act.

Exercises

Exercise 12: The Magical Act

This exercise is about recognizing the features that characterize a piece of communication as either official or unofficial, and attempting to take a piece of communication from one area to another.

Record a number of signs that you feel are characteristically unofficial marks. These may be photographs of graffiti tags or marks made by individuals very quickly or in an informal way.

Collect several pages of advertisements from magazines. Deconstruct one or two of these so you are clear about who the audience is and how the manufacturer or supplier wants to position itself. Think about the age group of the audience and the demographic. Is the product appealing to professional people? Is it expensive or affordable and accessible? Try to be clear about what the clues are: the way the image or illustration is presented, the use of words, the way the logo is drawn, the choice of typeface, and so on.

Your task is now to transfer the unofficial signs into official visual culture by using the information from the decoded advertisements. This might entail redrawing the unofficial marks as if they were logos for a particular demographic, reinterpreting the message as a studio photograph, or typesetting an original scrawled text as a magazine layout.

If you want to test the transfer, you can make a brief multiple-choice sheet to be used in short interviews. The interviewer might ask the reader to look at the images and tick a box that attributes the imagery to a particular type of company or to a particular audience.

Exercise 13: Visual Dialect

Create a text for a series of invitations to "formal" events. These could be real events or events that you have invented, such as an invitation to your graduation ceremony or an invitation to meet the president of the United States. Think about the type of words that you would use to characterize the formality of the occasion and a suitable venue for these events. Think now about what would be a very informal setting for an event like this, and visualize the invitation in a style that shifts the mood completely, perhaps with a different audience in mind. You might invite friends to your graduation ceremony in your garden shed or to meet the president of the United States in the supermarket car park or at the nearest bus stop. As you visualize the invitations for these new situations, try to ensure that the way you present visual signals captures the mood of the new venue while retaining the same basic text.

18. **P. Bourdieu**, "Intellectual Field and Creative Project" (1966), in *Knowledge and Control*, ed. M. F. D. Young (Collier-Macmillan, 1971).

19. **Bourdieu**, *Language and Symbolic Power*.

20. **L. Bloomfield**, *Language* (George Allen, 1958).

21. **Bourdieu**, *Language and Symbolic Power*.

22. **R. Galindo**, "Language Wars: The Ideological Dimensions of the Debates on Bilingual Education," *Bilingual Research Journal* 21, no. 2–3 (1997): 163–201.

23. **Galindo**, "Language Wars."

24. **Bourdieu**, *Language and Symbolic Power*.

25. **M. Livingstone**, *Pop Art* (Thames & Hudson, 1990).

26. **Livingstone**, *Pop Art*.

27. **Livingstone**, *Pop Art*.

28. **F. A. Horn**, *Lettering at Work* (The Studio Publications, 1955).

29. **Horn**, *Lettering at Work*.

30. **R. S. Hutchings**, *The Western Heritage of Type Design* (1963).

31. **P. Rand**, *A Designer's Art* (Yale University Press, 1985).

32. **M. Foucault**, *The History of Sexuality* (Pantheon Books, 1978).

33. **P. Bourdieu**, "Intellectual Field and Creative Project."

34. **C. V. Boundas**, *The Deleuze Reader* (Columbia University Press, 1993).

35. **J. L. Austin**, *How to Do Things with Words* (Oxford Paperbacks, 1955).

36. **M. Brake**, *Sociology of Youth Culture and Youth Subcultures* (Routledge & Kegan Paul, 1980).

37. **T. Manco**, *Stencil Graffiti* (Thames & Hudson, 2002).

38. **M. Fuller**, *Flyposter Frenzy* (Working Press, 1992).

39. **Manco**, *Stencil Graffiti*.

Chapter Six
Symbolic Creativity

Hyperinstitutionalization

6.1

Paul Willis claims there is a vibrant symbolic life and an active symbolic creativity in everyday life, everyday activities and expressions. He points us to the way in which young people's lives are actually full of expressions, signs, and symbols.

6.2

Paul Willis[40] introduces us to the idea of symbolic creativity by quoting statistics from the UK General Household Survey. Despite a huge effort to increase participation at traditional arts venues, the most recent survey[41] on well-being shows that young people put personal and informal cultural gestures before any form of "official" culture. Themes like technology, mobile phones, iPods, social networking sites, reality TV, celebrity gossip, and the right clothes, shoes, makeup, and hairstyle come out on top in terms of activities that help them form their identity. This supports Willis's assertion that the various genres that constitute high art are currently institutions that have no real relationship to young people and their lives. He argues that the arts establishment has done little to discourage the commonly held belief that

**6.1
James Jarvis, Ozzy.**

Illustration originally produced for *The Face* magazine.

**6.2
James Gosnold,
Four Horsemen of
the Apocalypse.**

Spot color illustration depicting a modern visual metaphor for the *Four Horsemen of the Apocalypse* taken from the Book of Revelation (after Jon McNaught).

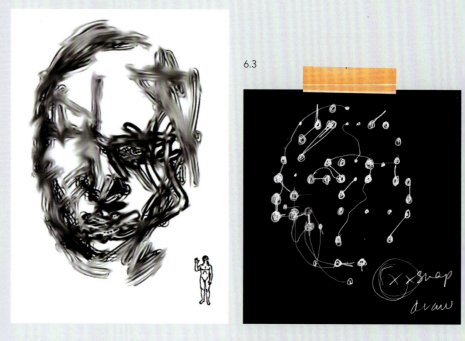

6.3

gallery-based art is special, heightened, and certainly not everyday. He contends that, in fact, these institutions of high art promote a fear of cultural decay in order to strengthen claims for subsidy and privilege. Against this, Willis claims there is a vibrant symbolic life and an active symbolic creativity in everyday life, everyday activities and expressions. He points us to the way in which young people's lives are actually full of expressions, signs, and symbols, despite their not being involved with the arts:

"the multitude of ways in which young people use, humanise, decorate and invest with meaning their common and immediate life spaces and social practices—personal styles and choice of clothes; selective and active use of music, TV, magazines; decoration of bedrooms; the rituals of romance and subcultural styles; the style, the banter and drama of friendship groups; music-making and dance."[42]

[Hyperinstitutionalization is] . . . a situation in which formal features, rather than a relevance to real-life concerns, become the guarantee of an aesthetic. The people who don't understand, the uncultured, simply lack the code and are seen (and may even see themselves) as ignorant or insensitive.

6.4

6.3–6.4
David Crow,
Megafamily.

Sketches and
development work
from the Megafamily
font.

It is the tendency of high art to distance itself from these things, insisting on prior educational knowledge, that leads to a complete dislocation of art from living contexts. This often results in what Willis calls hyperinstitutionalization—a situation in which formal features, rather than a relevance to real-life concerns, become the guarantee of an aesthetic. The people who don't understand, the uncultured, simply lack the code and are seen (and may even see themselves) as ignorant or insensitive.

He also returns to Bourdieu's notion of fields by placing the subsidized artist on the periphery of the field of symbolic creativity and the public at the center, reversing the traditional view. Willis maintains that this symbolic activity is not only vibrant but necessary because human beings are communicating as well as producing beings. While not all are productive, all are communicative. He stresses the necessity of symbolic work and offers the following definition:

"The application of human capacities to and through, on and with symbolic resources and raw materials (collections of signs and symbols—for instance the language as we inherit it, texts, images, films, songs, artifacts to produce meaning)." [43]

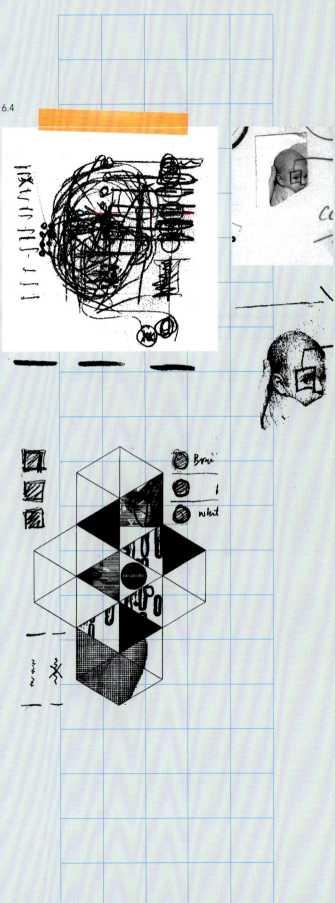

Play and Identity

Willis' definition is somewhat at odds with the English radical tradition of the 1920s and 1930s, which followed the ideas of people like William Morris, who stressed the dignity of labor in his equation: art = work/pleasure. Necessary work was, at this point, seen as human capacity applied through the action of tools on raw materials to produce goods or services (usually through wage labor). However, Willis notes that the mechanization of modern industry has made it impossible to find art in paid work, pointing to an extreme example in which a study of British factory workers found more opportunity for symbolic production in driving to work than there was to be found at work. This lack of opportunity for necessary symbolic work in the workplace highlights the importance of play in our individual expression. It is the informal rather than the formal situation that offers us freedom and choice in symbolic activity, and increasingly this is where our necessary symbolic work takes place. According to Willis, the increased importance of play has been reflected in the huge growth of commercialized leisure, with opinion divided about whether or not commercial status devalues cultural currency.

Willis separates symbolic creativity from material production and suggests that it be seen as symbolic production. He outlines four elements needed for necessary symbolic work:

1. *The primary communication tool of language, which enables interaction and allows us to assess our impact on others and their impact on us.*

2. *The active body (according to Willis this is the site of signs and symbols).*

3. *The drama of roles and rituals which we perform with others.*

4. *The practice of symbolic production (where language is both the raw materials and the tools) bringing about new ways of producing meaning.*

"In many ways this is a question of cultural survival for many young people." [44]

6.5
Ian Wright, Bob Dylan.

A portrait of the musician constructed from button badges.

This is how we produce and how we reproduce our own individual identities, who we are now and who we could become. It also places these identities in time and place and defines membership in groups such as race, gender, age, and religion.

Willis maintains that symbolic creativity is intrinsically attached to energy, feelings, excitement, and psychic movement. He believes this to be the basis of confidence.

Having outlined what symbolic creativity is and what we need in order for it to take place, Willis then offers a number of examples of what is produced by symbolic creativity. He suggests that this is how we produce and reproduce our own individual identities—who we are now and who we could become. It also places these identities in time and place and defines membership in groups, such as race, gender, age, and religion. It also empowers us with the expectation of being able to change the world we live in and to make our mark on it. Willis sees these activities as transitive, in that we are constantly experimenting with these expressions of identity and have a cultural sense of which haircut, language, or music (for example) works most economically for ourselves.

Willis stresses the importance of this aspect of symbolic production. He points out how young people in particular feel marginalized by the constructed visions of youth supplied by our society through institutions, advertising, magazines, and television, as they perceive the difference between how they are told they should be and how they actually are. Studies of football (soccer) hooligans in the United Kingdom also point to the necessity for disenfranchised young people to define their identity in opposition to existing constructs.

"The struggle begins when they see many of the things that seem routine to the rest of us as ways of devaluing them. . . . If they are to have any significance, their lives must be self-constructed and made significant with the use of home-made materials."[45]

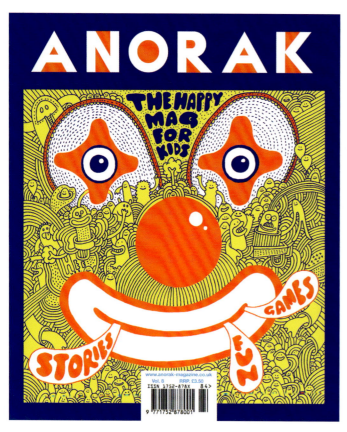

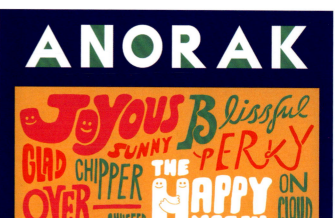

6.6

6.7

6.6–6.10
Creator: Supermundane – Rob Lowe
Title: Anorak Magazine
Exemplifies: Symbolic Creativity

This magazine is packed full of ideas for odd things to do, cool things to wear, chocolate recipes, and surreal takes on the world around us. Its unique visual style complements its anarchic approach to the content. The exclusive use of drawn imagery and absence of conventional typography helps to create a distinct community of readers who share the same reference points. It talks directly to children and creates a world where the everyday choices that we make to express ourselves are offered to children of all ages.

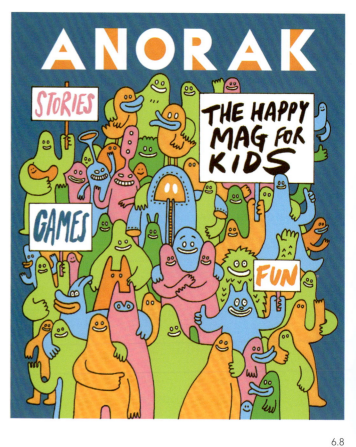

6.8

6.9

6.10

6.11

6.11–6.13
Creator: Kate Moross
Title: Make Your Own Luck
Exemplifies: Symbolic Creativity

An exhibition in a small independent London Gallery to coincide with the publication of a book with the same title. The show is full of everyday items that people commonly use to express their creativity as individuals and communicate their identity. Clothing, prints, books, records, jewelry, and lollipops all jostle for attention in a layout that resembles a boutique rather than an exhibition. The context of the project is as important as the visual language used. An event in a carefully chosen venue is a very important sign, and the use of a small independent gallery helps the author to blur the worlds of art, design, and lifestyle.

6.12

6.13

6.14–6.17
Art Direction: Designers Republic
Illustrations: Students and Staff from
Manchester School of Art
Title: Hoarding
Exemplifies: Symbolic Creativity

6.18
Art Direction: Designers Republic
Illustrations: Students and Staff from
Manchester School of Art
Title: Invitations to End of Year Show
Exemplifies: Symbolic Creativity

The hoarding surrounding the extension to
the Manchester School of Art was the site for a
mass expression of individual expression. The
hoarding featured more than 120 self-portraits
made by students and staff from the school. A
life-sized full-length portrait of each participant
was the basic canvas for a long line of images that
expressed the creativity and personal identity of
the individuals that make up the school. Many
of the illustrators used clothes, accessories, or
gestures to express themselves. One photograph
shows a close-up of some of the portraits
alongside a site worker whose own identity is
casually expressed through his clothing, gestures,
and stance as he proudly takes his place among
the student portraits.
A series of cut-up figures using a number of the
portraits were used to promote the end-of-year
shows, expressing the breadth, diversity, and
personal creativity of the individuals in the show.

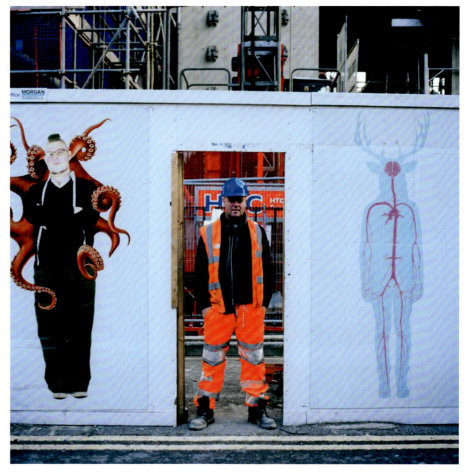

6.14

6.15

6.16

6.17

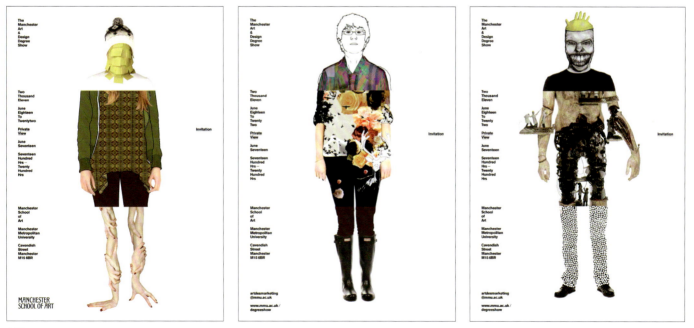

6.18

6.19

a BALL
x WALL
1 FOOT
2 FACE

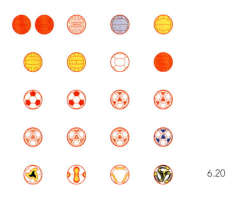

6.20

6.21

6.19–6.22
Creators: Staff from Liverpool School of Art and Design
Title: I Don't Love Soccer Because Soccer Has Never Loved Me
Exemplifies: Symbolic Creativity/Anchorage/ Paradigm

6.19 Ben Jones (Ball. Wall. Foot. Face)
6.20 Jon Spencer (Ball Games: Football)
6.21 Chris Rodenhurst (The Crisis Deepens)
6.22 Seel Garside (Formations)

A collection of artworks produced in response to an essay titled "The World Cup and Its Pomps," written in 1978 by the famous Italian semiotician, intellectual, and writer Umberto Eco and published in his collection of essays *Travels in Hyperreality* (1986). Eco links football (soccer) "with the absence of purpose and the vanity of all things," questioning the banality of its punditry, its inherent prejudice and exclusivity, and its (a)political morality. The essay concludes with Eco asking rhetorically, "Is the armed struggle possible on World Cup Sunday . . . Is revolution possible on a football Sunday?"

As a totality, the collection and the resulting book can be read as a collective expression of identity from the contributors. Their shared frustration with the media coverage of the World Cup is translated differently by each of the contributors in a visual panorama that allows each of them to express their identity within this common framework.

There are a number of semiotic devices to look for among the works. In "The Crisis Deepens," the text functions as relay text, supplying the narrative as a conversation to an ambiguous scene frozen in time as a still (see also "Anchorage and Relay" in Chapter 4). In "Ball Games: Football," the drawings of balls are a perfect example of a linguistic paradigm where the units in the set have something in common yet are obviously different from other units in the set (see also "Paradigm" in Chapter 2).

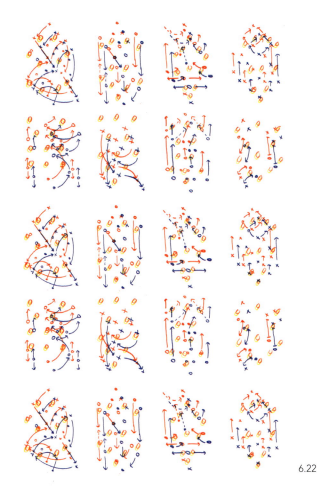

6.22

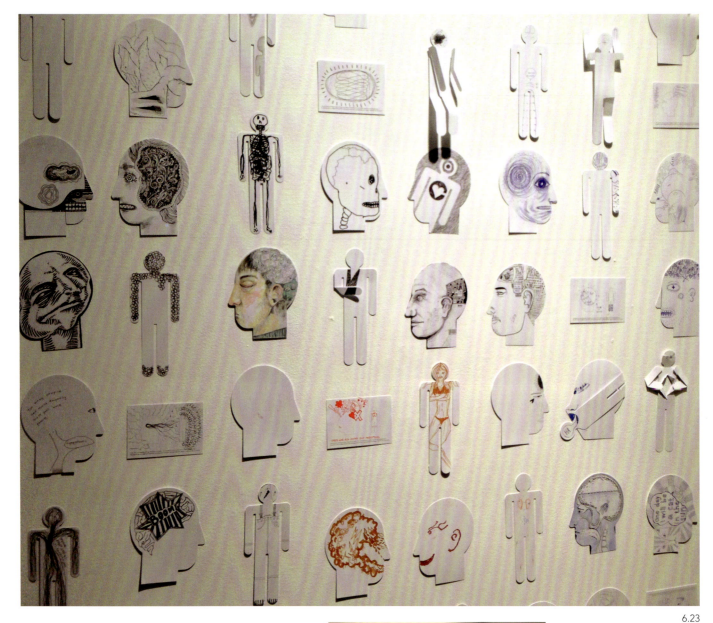

6.23

6.23–6.25
Creator: Ashley Booth and Linda Lien
Title: Pictogram-me: A visualization of a difficult life
Exemplifies: Symbolic Creativity

Pictogram-me are interested in using direct effective visual tools to communicate socially significant messages. They work with some of those who have a difficult life, either as an individual or as part of a group that face challenges in their community. By asking the participants to describe their lives through visualizing and storytelling, Pictogram-me transform the events of their everyday lives into a series of pictograms that facilitate self expression and help to develop an interactive narrative to a wide audience.

6.24

6.25

Pictogram-me

Exercises

Exercise 14: Identity

Choose an individual you know well enough to be able to spend some time in their workplace and/or home. Preferably, this should be someone who does not work in the creative industries and is not the same age as you. Make a body of visual research based around how this individual expresses their identity. Look for instances in which they are not actively trying to express themselves but nevertheless tell you a lot about their attitude and outlook on life. Use your camera, make sound recordings, make drawings, and try not to determine the outcome during the research stage. The task is to bring the documentary research together in a digestible format that functions as a celebration of your chosen subject. The format may relate directly to your subject or could be an established documentary format, such as a small booklet, a video, or a blog. Please be sensitive towards your subject in how you publish the work, and remember to get permission from them beforehand.

40. **Willis**, *Common Culture*.

41. UK Office for National Statistics, *General Household Survey* (1983–86).

42. **Willis**, *Common Culture*.

43. **Willis**, *Common Culture*.

44. **Willis**, *Common Culture*.

45. **P. Marsh, E. Rosser, and R. Harré**, *The Rules of Disorder* (Routledge & Kegan Paul, 1978).

Chapter Seven
Junk and Culture

Dirt and Taboo

Mary Douglas points out that dirt is the by-product of a system of order. Dirt has been rejected in a process of classification as the elements that are out of place. Douglas argues that if we look at what counts as dirt, then we can begin to understand and identify the system that rejects it.

Our ideas about what constitutes dirt are part of a symbolic system of signs, which has clear categories used to organize the signs into a hierarchy of importance or use:

> *"Shoes are not dirty in themselves, but it is dirty to place them on the dining table; food is not dirty in itself, but it is dirty to leave cooking utensils in the bedroom, or food bespattered on clothing; similarly bathroom equipment in the drawing room; clothing lying on chairs; outdoor things indoors; upstairs things downstairs; underclothing appearing where overclothing should be and so on. In short, our pollution behaviour is the reaction which condemns any object or idea likely to confuse or contradict cherished classifications."*[47]

"Where there is dirt there is a system."[46]

**7.1
Joe Briggs Price &
Ian Walker, Doll.**

A discarded doll that makes an uneasy image for the viewer as the innocence of childhood is sharply contrasted with a perception of rejection and danger.

7.1

7.2

7.3

Douglas shows us that the threat of danger is often used as a justification for social convention. We might well be endangering our health or that of our family by not throwing out an item of chipped crockery. Dangerous germs may lurk in the chip, ready to make us ill. She points out that what's really under threat, however, is the semiotics of ordered social conventions, which are the agreed practice in our society.

To understand why something has been rejected, we need to rebuild a picture of the systems of signification that lie beneath the decision to reject it from the system. In this sense, then, we can see that the study of dirt or rubbish is a semiotic study.

For example, to understand what is currently fashionable in typography, you would need to look at what has been discarded as unfashionable. This helps to define the category and describe what is at the margins of fashionably acceptable.

In Chapter 5, we looked at the idea of official and unofficial language. We have also discussed the interplay between the two and how one cannot exist without the other. In order to comprehend what constitutes legitimate language, we need to know what has been rejected as inappropriate in any given situation. Unofficial language is the dirt in a system that has rejected it in favor of an accepted and legitimate language choice:

"As we know it, dirt is essentially disorder." [18]

Since order and pattern are made from a limited selection of elements, there is an implication that pattern is restricted in some way. Disorder, the enemy of pattern, could then be considered unlimited. Disorder has no pattern in itself, but its potential for making pattern is infinite. Douglas argues that in the first instance we recognize that disorder destroys existing patterns but also that it has huge potential. This leads us to view disorder as a symbol of both danger and power.

7.2–7.3
Jack Hatton,
Lego and Marble.

Two children's toys recovered from an archaelogical dig that evoke an emotional response around loss and childhood memory.

Rubbish Theory

In his essay "Rubbish Theory," Jonathan Culler[49] invites us to consider the rubbish that is not particularly dirty or taboo. This is the rubbish that we all have stored away in spare rooms, garages, and lofts: old football programs, comics, postcards, tickets, and coins. Some of this is rubbish we have inherited: my father's pen and a watch that doesn't work; my grandfather's penknife and ration book from the 1940s. These objects were all edited from a wider set of rubbish of which some things were kept and others rejected. If dirt is evidence of a system of classification, then how, asks Culler, do we read these cupboards full of everyday rubbish?

Much of this material functions as souvenirs. Perhaps it signifies for us an experience we have had or something we have seen, which in time will become a significant part of our life. Visual constructions often use these sorts of items to signify memory in some way. You may find it disrespectful to consider mementos, especially those handed down by your parents, as rubbish. However, in most cases, the collected material has no economic value nor any practical use. For these reasons we can consider it rubbish.

Semiotic Categories of Objects

This relationship between rubbish and value is clarified by Michael Thompson in his essay also titled "Rubbish Theory." Thompson[50] identifies three semiotic categories of objects that have a direct relation to economic value.

Transient cultural objects have a finite life span, and their economic value decreases over time. Foodstuffs are an obvious example of transient objects, but the term could also refer to objects that are susceptible to the whims of fashion. This illustrates that it is not only the physical properties of an object that categorize it; there is also a social dimension that attributes value based on the values in our society.

The value of durable cultural objects is maintained or even increased over time. These objects have no finite life span; they may even be considered as having an infinite life span. Antiques are a good example of durable objects. This category also includes items that may have started life as fairly inexpensive and common but have become durable because there is a collector's marketplace for them.

7.4
Durable Object

The Mercedes-Benz motor car is an example of what could be described as a durable object, whose value is maintained or, in some cases, increased over a period of time.

7.4

Certain recordings, for example, have more value now than they did when new, as do commemorative items from historical events, such as a key ring from the Queen's coronation.

In brand advertising, many objects are presented in a way that reinforces their durable qualities. Mercedes-Benz, Timberland, and Rolex are all brands whose products are deliberately bound up in the notion of durability.

Thompson points out that those who have wealth or power will strive to keep their objects in the durable category and ensure that the transient objects of others remain so. This is a necessary step because we know it is possible for objects to shift from one category to another, and the transfer of economic value follows this shift.

To explain how this change is possible, Thompson identifies a third, less obvious category. This category contains objects that have an unchanging value of zero. Thompson outlines a scenario in which a transient object gradually loses value until it is worthless. It remains in this valueless state until someone rediscovers it and transforms it into a durable object. We

have all experienced revivalist fashion coming from an utterly unfashionable period. Styles that have only recently waned in popularity rarely make a successful comeback, whereas a style that has been discarded always has the potential for being fashionable again. Thompson's "Rubbish Theory" describes how transient cultural objects can only move to the durable category once they have been considered rubbish.

Buying a classic car or a piece of antique furniture is about buying into the semiotic idea of durable objects. The way we treat our objects is also a sign of which category we believe they belong in. We might cherish and maintain our classic car, carefully restoring the most banal detail to its original state. However, if we have a new model that declines in value, we are at some point likely to let things go wrong if we plan to replace it. It is simply not worth any further investment. We may eventually pay a scrap metal dealer to tow away our worthless vehicle. It may sit untouched for years, only to be rediscovered two or three decades later as a classic and be bought by a collector for restoration.

Those who have wealth or power will strive to keep their objects in the durable category and ensure that the transient objects of others remain so.

This theory appears to draw inspiration from *Purity and Danger,* where Mary Douglas[51] poses the question of whether dirt, which is normally destructive, can ever be considered creative. In her exploration of this question, she describes two stages that dirt must go through to achieve creative symbolism. First, in the process of imposing order, dirt must be differentiated as being out of place. Dirt is seen to be unwanted, but it still has some identity in that it can be recognized as the unwanted item. Over time, however, this identity gradually disappears, until the unwanted item becomes part of the general mass of rubbish.

Douglas states that as long as there is no identity, then dirt is not dangerous. At this stage it is not differentiated in any way, just as it was before it became classified as dirt. This completes a cycle in which dirt moves from a non-differentiated state to a differentiated state (recognized and classified as dirt) and then finally back to its original state of non-differentiation as part of the general mass of discarded dirt. She argues that it is in this formless state that dirt can function as a sign of growth as much as a sign of decay. The argument concludes that everything that applies to the purifying role of water in religious symbolism could also be applied to dirt.

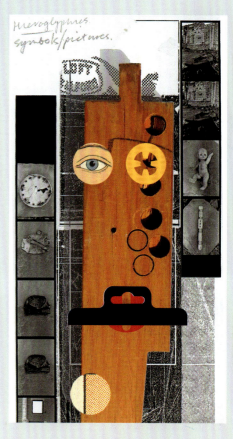

"Earth should be a cloud of dust, a soil of bones,
With no room even for our skeletons.
It is wasted time to think of it, to count its grains,
When all are alike and there is no difference in them."[52]

7.5

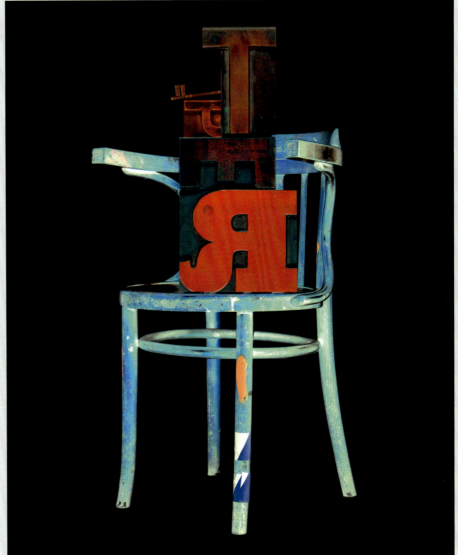

The transient object gradually loses value until it is worthless.
It remains in this valueless state until someone rediscovers it and transforms it into a durable object.

7.5
David Crow, St.Peter.

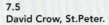

An old chair rescued from a skip becomes the centrepiece for an image that features a portrait of a religious figure.

Rubbish
as a Resource

7.6

As we have already seen in Chapter 5, there are clear hierarchies at play in cultural production. The fine arts are generally considered a more significant practice than design disciplines. The work produced by each of these areas is also considered differently in terms of their importance as cultural objects.

In his essay "Rubbish Theory," Jonathan Culler describes two types of cultural artifact. First, there are artifacts that are part of the practical world: utilitarian objects, such as newspapers, magazines, and television. These are considered transient cultural objects. Then there are artifacts that have no obvious purpose and are presented as being separate from commercial or practical concerns.

These are part of our world of leisure and are broadly categorized as part of our cultural heritage. These we see as durables. Culler points out that cultural rubbish has become a valuable resource in the visual arts. He cites the example of Carl Andre's *Bricks,* bought by the Tate Gallery in 1972. This pile of common household bricks would have been considered rubbish by many who saw it at the time. They may well have had a similar pile of unwanted bricks in their own backyard. However, the museum that bought the work saw it as part of the category of durables. The work had been "authorized" by the museum, and arrangements of common rubbish made by recognized artists became collectable again.

A marketplace for similar artifacts had been established, and *Bricks* increased in value. More recently, the same gallery came under fire from the popular press over the display of Tracey Emin's *Bed,* which was surrounded by an assortment of household rubbish. Although there is little concern shown when transient objects become rubbish,

> #1 { **Offset Lithography** ...used to shift an unwanted and discarded book in the general direction of durability and value once more. Issued in an edition of one.
>
> **Reintroduction 1**
> David Crow

A debate often ensues in which those who wish to establish an object as durable draw on the discourse of legitimate language to justify the transition.

7.7

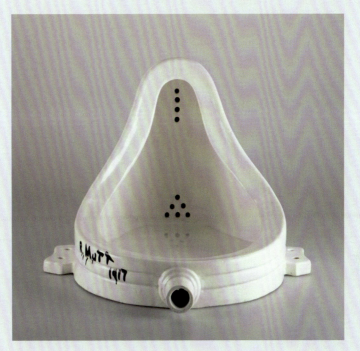

the transformation from rubbish to durable always provokes a strong reaction. Those who wish to establish an object as a durable often draw on the discourse of legitimate language to justify the transition.

There are a number of earlier examples of this transition, when an equally vociferous outcry heralded their appearance. If we look at the self-proclaimed anti-art Dada movement, there are numerous examples that use rubbish as a resource to change the way we approach the notion of what constitutes art. Marcel Duchamp's sculptures from the early part of the twentieth century (such as *Bicycle Wheel, Hat Rack,* and *Urinal*) were all discarded functional objects that became durables. These are now cited as classic pieces of art, serving as inspiration for generations of visual artists.

**7.6
Re-introduced.**

A page from an artist's book by the author where a discarded library book about offset lithography is taken apart and overprinted using a litho press in an attempt to shift the value from rubbish to durable.

**7.7
Marcel Duchamp,
Fountain,** 1917.

7.6

7.6–7.8
Creator: Hazel Jones
Title: Gooseberry Squeezer
Title: Plumptious Gooseberry Medal
Exemplifies: Rubbish to Durable

These objects were made for a group exhibition at the Tatton Park Agricultural Show in England. Hazel awarded herself this medal along with a certificate for the best gooseberry she grew this year. She also felt the gooseberry needed a device to test how "plumptious" it was. The objects form part of an extensive collection of discarded items. With blogs devoted to categories such as "How to Market Bent Wire" or "Loose Bits and Lost Buttons," Jones demonstrates the ability of the visual arts to transform the economic and cultural value of worthless objects by placing them in a different context and in a different dialogue.

7.7

7.8

7.9
Creator: David Crow
Title: Old King Cole – Digital Installation
Exemplifies: Rubbish to Durable

A section from a seamless digital wallpaper installation at the Museum of Architecture and Design, Ljubljana, Slovenia. The title refers to Sir Henry Cole who in the mid-1800s was the Secretary of the Department of Science in Art and Director of the South Kensington Museum, now the Victoria and Albert Museum, in London. He was reportedly a difficult individual who was often described as a monster by many of his contemporaries. "Old King Cole," as he became known, played a leading role in the Great Exhibition of 1851, which featured, among many other things, a series of household products such as ceramics and wallpapers, which were widely criticized by designers at the time. Their primary concern was the fall in design standards and the popularity of these supposedly debased and ugly products. This led to the involvement of Sir Henry Cole, who took it upon himself to educate the people of England in matters of taste.
The installation uses a number of items that are apparently worthless, such as an old sawhorse, an old chair, an old mallet, and a number of kitsch decorative plates, as the key visual elements in the work. The presence of the hand of the designer and the context of the work in a design museum become signs of the increasing cultural value of the objects as they move from worthless objects to integral parts of a cultural artifact with a degree of durability.

7.10

7.10
Creator: Rodrigo de Filippis
Title: Como Un Souvenir
Exemplifies: Rubbish to Durable

A variety of found images and discarded ephemera are recombined by Filippis to create this print. The worthless scraps of imagery are given value by the artist's placing them in a new context. In bringing together a set of disparate, worthless objects in an arrangement made by an artist, the work becomes authorized and valuable again. The transfer of value from the artist to the object is underlined by the presence of hand-drawn elements that personalize the work and function as the artist's signature. The future value of works like these will then depend on the discourse that happens around them. Reviews, exhibitions, and publications featuring the work all contribute to a value system that collectively determines their worth.

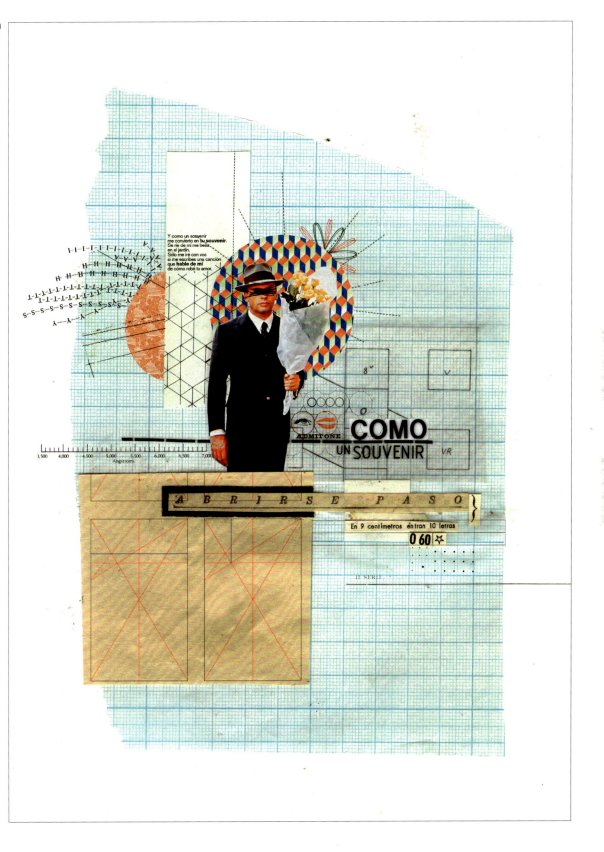

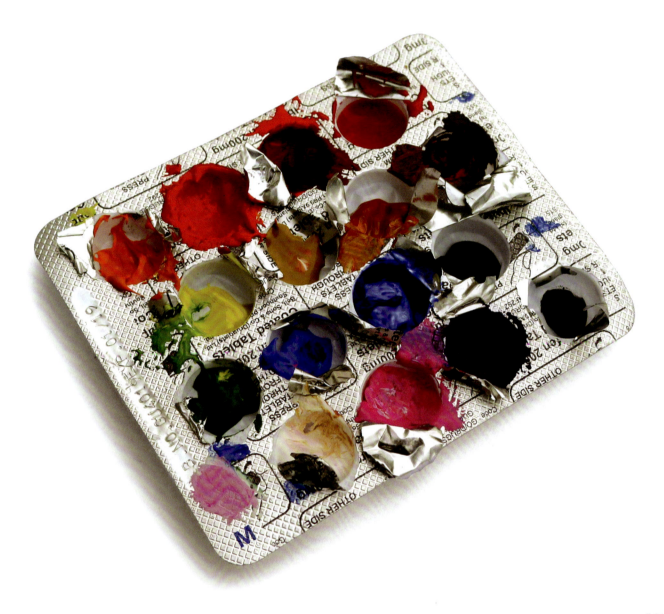

7.11
Creator: Joe Magee
Title: Pill Palette
Exemplifies: Rubbish to Durable

Create Gloucestershire, an arts incubator group, wanted an image to accompany a piece titled *An Artist a Day Keeps the Doctor Away*, a discussion about the relationship between art and health, and how a daily "dose" of art can help build and sustain a healthy and meaningful life. The pill packet is a familiar mass-produced item that is discarded without thought as rubbish the moment the valuable contents are gone. In this design, the worthless object becomes a palette with direct associations to the durable world of the fine arts.

The act of popping out a pill from a packet elicits a particular feeling in the user—one of impending relief or a road to well-being. The fact that, in this image, the packet contains paints is disconcerting and makes the connection clear between the anticipation of relief and art. The bright colors subvert what we expect in the normally monotone packaging and contents, adding an edge because it's dangerous to consider pills to be fun—but art can be anything it wants.

Exercises

Exercise 15: Rubbish/Cultural Objects

Make an exhibition catalogue to accompany your own "Museum of the Ordinary." To do this, you will need to document a collection of objects that are overlooked by almost everyone who sees or experiences them. These could be objects that are very personal and signify a particular memory, despite being worthless in monetary terms. Alternatively, you might consider the museum to be your immediate urban or rural environment. In this instance, you will also need to help the reader find the "exhibits." Your role is to explore how you can present these objects in a way that gives them a cultural value that belies their ordinariness and elevates them to exhibits, either for their historic interest or as found-art objects.

Exercise 16: Worthless/Durable

Go to your local thrift store and purchase the cheapest secondhand book you can find. Make a series of interventions, subtractions or additions, to this book to transform it into an original artist book artifact. Don't forget to sign the book to signify that it is now a prized cultural object.

46. **M. Douglas**, *Purity and Danger* (Routledge & Kegan Paul, 1966).

47. **Douglas**, *Purity and Danger.*

48. **Douglas**, *Purity and Danger.*

49. **J. Culler**, "Rubbish Theory," *in Framing the Sign*, ed. J. Culler (Basil Blackwell, 1988).

50. **M. Thompson**, "Rubbish Theory: The Creation and Destruction of Value" (1979), in *Framing the Sign*, ed. J. Culler (Basil Blackwell, 1988).

51. **Douglas**, *Purity and Danger.*

52. **S. Sitwell**, Agamemnon's Tomb (1972), in *Douglas, Purity and Danger.*

Chapter Eight
Open Work

What Is Open Work?

The term "open work" comes from a book of the same name written by Umberto Eco,[53] a philosopher and semiotician born in Piedmont, Italy, in 1932. First published in 1962, the book anticipated important developments in contemporary art and remains a significant piece of writing today. In particular, Eco was interested in the relationship between the author of a work of art and the reader.

Like Peirce[54] before him, Eco places particular emphasis on the role of the reader as an important part of the creative process. As readers, we receive a work of art as the end product of an intended message. This message has been assembled and organized by the author in a way that makes it possible for readers to reassemble it for themselves as the author intended. However, we know that the reader's background affects the way that the message is reassembled. The overall meaning of the message may be constant, but each of us brings an individual perspective to the reading based on our culture, background, and experiences.

Eco prefers the term "encyclopedia," rather than the more common term "code," to describe the transfer of meaning through the use of signs. For Eco, a code implies a one-to-one transfer of meaning like a dictionary definition, whereas encyclopedia suggests that there are a number of interrelated interpretations and readers must negotiate their own path through the network of possibilities. Although Eco sees an openness in the reading of signs, he does not suggest that there are an infinite number of readings. Rather, he describes a situation in which the work of art is addressed to an ideal reader who will select from the suggested readings of the work. The ideal reader is not a perfect reader who interprets the work exactly as the author intended, but a reader who is awake to the possibilities that the work contains.

Eco sees art as a performance[55] because each reader finds a new interpretation, and much of his writing focuses on musical performances as examples of the open work. Composers such as Stockhausen are cited because the work is open in a more obvious way than in the visual arts. The composer supplies the musicians with a kit of parts, with the invitation to interpret the material for themselves. In this way, the work is obviously incomplete until the reader is involved. The freedom on the part of the reader—in this case, the musician—is conscious and explicit. Indeed, by asking musicians to interpret the work in their own way, the artist invites them to ask why they would want to work in this way. What is the conceptual framework for this piece?

In the visual arts, there has been a shift towards a greater personal involvement on the part of the reader. Along with a greater degree of formal innovation has come a greater degree of ambiguity. When Eco published *The Open Work,* the art world was dominated by developments such as abstract expressionism and action painting, movements that questioned our traditional views on representation and meaning. It called for the reader to work harder to find meaning.

Information and Meaning

If a newsflash tells me that tomorrow the sun will rise, I have been given very little information as I could have worked this out for myself. If, however, the newsflash tells me that the sun will not rise, then I have a lot of information as this is a highly improbable event.

In an attempt to help define what he means by openness, Eco uses the mathematical science of information theory to measure the relationship between the amount of information that the reader receives and the openness of a work. It is important to note that he sees information as something different from meaning or message. He suggests that the amount of information contained in a message depends on the probability of the reader's already knowing the content of the message before it is received. If a newsflash tells me that tomorrow the sun will rise, I have been given very little information as I could have worked this out for myself. If, however, the newsflash tells me that the sun will not rise, then I have a lot of information as this is a highly improbable event. Eco presents a mathematical formula, reproduced here for reference, which essentially proposes that the amount of information contained in a message is inversely proportional to the probability or predictability of the message.

For Eco, contemporary art is highly unpredictable because it often dismisses the established semiotic conventions and rules that preceded it. Eco argues that contemporary art contains much higher amounts of information, though not necessarily more meaning, by virtue of its radical nature. More conventional forms of communication—such as the road sign, for example, or figurative painting—may carry more distinct meaning but much less information.

Eco also points out that the amount of information contained in a message is affected by another factor: our confidence in the source of the message. The example he uses is the traditional Western Christmas card: a seasonal greeting exchanged each year between families and friends. To receive a Christmas card from the secret police would be very different from receiving a card from a favorite aunt. Although the message is essentially the same (Merry Christmas), the amount of information varies hugely because of the improbability of the source. Similarly, if a landlord were to tell me an apartment had damp problems before I rented it, I would be more inclined to believe him because he has nothing to gain by fabricating this message.

It is tempting to assume that information and meaning are the same thing. However, we can see from these examples that the amount of information is greater when the content or the source is improbable. Compare this to the statement "Christmas is an annual festival." This has a very clear and direct meaning with no ambiguity, yet it doesn't add to our existing knowledge. In other words, although the communicative value is high, the amount of information is low.

don't

The amount of information contained in a message

believe

depends on where it originates and on its probablility

a word

Openness and the Visual Arts

Eco focuses on the painting styles of abstract expressionism and action painting, which were current when *The Open Work* was written. He describes how these can be seen on one level as the latest in a series of experiments to introduce movement into painting. However, there are a number of ways in which movement is signified in the visual arts. The use of repetition and the addition of trace lines around an image have long been established as signifiers of movement. These are signs that work on fixed structures, and they have been around for as long as we have used images to communicate. In these cases, the nature of the sign itself is not affected, merely the position of the signs relative to each other. For example, if we repeat a figure a number of times across the same work but in different settings, we begin to describe a timeline and we see the figure in a changing narrative. Compare this with the ambiguous forms of the Impressionist painters, the blurred images that became possible with the introduction of the camera, or the gestural marks of abstract expressionism.

In these examples, the nature of the sign itself has become ambiguous, if not the forms they signify. We still read the forms in the paintings as people or buildings or bridges, but according to Eco they have acquired an inner vibrancy. The reader is now conscious of the movement of light around the subjects.

Similarly, with the gestural marks of abstract expressionism, we are reading the way the mark is made— the action that has left this mark as evidence. The open work offers readers a field of open possibilities. They can choose their own viewpoint, decide for themselves what is foreground and background, and make their own connections between different parts of what they see. An obvious example of this is the sculptural mobiles of artists like Alexander Calder. Theoretically, the work offers the possibility that no two experiences of it will be the same.

The question one invariably asks of work like this is whether or not it communicates. Is the work legible, and how do we stop it descending into a chaotic visual noise or a complete communicative silence?

Openness and Information

Eco is interested in the tension between the information offered to the reader and the level of comprehension needed for the work to be interpreted. Can the reader detect the intentions of the author of the work? Is an agreement between the two discernible? Some types of visual communication clearly need structure and order—signs that, because of their practical application, need to be read and understood quickly. In situations where speed of communication is important, pictograms bridge the gap between the technical world and language. In other cases, where the practical application is less important, there are signs that merely seek to give information as opposed to meaning.

Another way of looking at these signs is to see them as seeking to deliver not a single meaning but an abundance of possible meanings. In contemporary art and design, there are many examples of works that deliberately seek to avoid what Eco calls "the laws of probability that govern common language."[56] In fact,

he points out that contemporary art draws its value from this deviation from common structures. If we spill ink on a blank sheet of paper, we are presented with a random image that has no order. No particular direction is given to the reader in terms of how to interpret the image. If we then fold the paper in two and transfer the image onto both sides of the paper, we now have an image with some order.

In this case, the order is symmetry—a simple form of probability. The reader now has some visual reference points that can be connected together to suggest a way of reading the image. Although the image still offers readers a good deal of freedom in terms of interpretation, they now have some direction. If we were to shred the paper, make paper pulp and roll it out to dry as a sheet again, there would be a huge number of dots and marks across the surface of the paper. The reader could begin to connect these marks in an infinite number of ways, but there would be no discernible direction for the reader.

8.1
Ian Wright, Heads.

The skull and crossbones is a symbol that, because of its practical application (poisonous chemicals, electric pylons), needs to be read and understood quickly. In situations where speed of communication is important, these pictograms bridge the gap between the technical world and language. The heads by Ian Wright work on quite a different level; in this instance, readers are invited to bring their own meaning and character to the drawings.

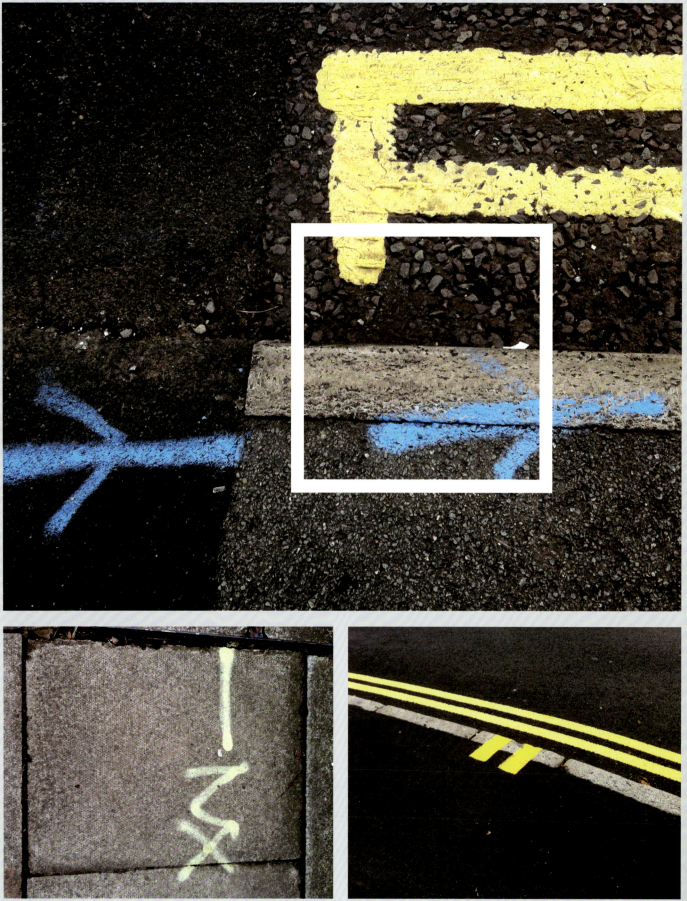

8.2

A piece of discarded material can become an artifact once it has been framed.

The image is now extremely open; it contains a maximum amount of information but is utterly meaningless. We are not likely to make one reading of the information above another. What we have is the visual equivalent of white noise. This excess of possibilities does not increase the information but denies it altogether. It doesn't communicate. Eco uses this as evidence that

> *"the richest form of communication—richest because most open—requires a delicate balance permitting the merest order within the maximum disorder."*[57]

He maintains that this is a characteristic of any visual communication that wants to be understood but also wants to allow a degree of freedom to the reader. He points out how the intention of the author may be enough to give the work a value. As we saw in Chapter 7, a piece of discarded material can become an artifact once it has been framed. Our pavements and roadways are peppered with cracks and holes. Some of these are framed with brightly colored squares painted by highway agencies to mark their priority for repair. This visual sign shows us that these cracks have been chosen over other cracks; it calls attention to them. Merely by being isolated, they have become artifacts.

8.2

Much of what an artist does is to make choices. By choosing to isolate a particular part of a pattern, we immediately make it an artifact.

Form and Openness

Eco reassures us that the informal sign does not mark the death of form in the visual arts, but proposes instead a new flexible form—a field of possibilities. The gestural marks and spatters of abstract painting stimulate viewers to make their own connections in the work. Reading the original gesture that leaves this mark, is fixed by this mark, is in this mark, will lead us eventually to the intention of the person who made the mark. According to Eco, it is this underlying intention that distinguishes a work of art from the patterns of the cracked pavement. The marks are the signifier of the gesture but not a symbolic sign for the gesture. The mark does not merely stand for the action. The gesture and the sign are fused together.

Unlike symbolic signs, which belong to a defined set of signs and whose meaning we have learned (like road signs or letters of the alphabet), these abstract marks need interpretation. There is no predetermined collection of these signs. They could be considered analogue codes rather than digital codes, like music or the gestural movements of dance. Eco argues that allowing readers to freely associate the signs enables them to enjoy the experience of doing this while simultaneously enjoying the aesthetics of the signs. Readers search for as many possible associations as they can in a game of pleasure and surprise, trying to interpret the intentions of the author as they do so.

Open work in the visual arts is, according to Eco, a guarantee of communication with added pleasure. The two things are connected together in a way not to be found in the reading of more conventional signs. When we read a road sign whose meaning we have learned, we read the message but rarely do we marvel at the aesthetics of the sign. Only those of us with a particularly strong industrial aesthetic would enjoy the effectiveness of the way the sign is made. Openness is pleasure. Our visual culture invites us to view the world as a world of possibilities.

> The mark does not merely stand for the action—it is the action. The gesture and the sign are fused together.

Openness is pleasure

8.3

8.3
Creator: Emily Forgot
Title: Caged Parents/ Title: Boy Pigeon
Exemplifies: Open Work

These decorated ceramics draw on a tradition that places them as domestic objects with special status in the home. They are often displayed rather than used and can commemorate events, act as souvenirs of a place, or celebrate a particular individual, usually an establishment figure.
These particular plates challenge viewers to find their own meaning as the central characters are combined with unexpected elements in a relationship that exists outside of our everyday experience. The scale of the elements has been altered and the characters rendered anonymous in silhouette form in a similar way to that of twentieth-century surrealists like René Magritte. The sheer economy of elements and economy of color force us to focus on the relationship between the signifiers. As a narrative, they are open and much closer to poetry than prose. The resulting poetic composition creates an emotional reaction that challenges viewers to make the associations for themselves based on the meaning they bring to the work, flavored by their own life experience.

8.4–8.5
Creator: Edward Carvalho Monaghan
Title: I Can't Get Over You/ Take Up Thy Stethoscope And Walk
Exemplifies: Open Work

Edward's work doesn't draw on obvious visual references, which makes the meaning difficult for the viewer to fix. Although Edward cites psychedelic music and the work of avant garde filmmaker Alejandro Jodorowsky as strong influences, he reinterprets these influences in a very individual way with his own internal logic and makes images that are difficult to decode in an objective way. However, this is also what makes the work so exciting as it pulls together imagery in such unusual combinations, giving you glimpses of an abstracted fragment of something you think you recognize—but you can't be sure. As this happens, viewers bring their own experiences and cultural background to the work and begin to seek out associations that make sense to them individually. The pleasure is in this personal search for meaning among a set of open signs.

8.4

8.5

8.6

8.6–8.7
Creator: David Crow with Media LAB
Title: BT Art Box
Exemplifies: Open Work

This remodeled version of the classic British telephone box was part of a series commissioned to celebrate the twenty-fifth anniversary of the charity ChildLine; the boxes were sited in busy public spaces across the city of London. The box houses an LED light curtain linked to two hidden cameras and connected via bespoke software coded for this application. Passers-by would be captured as silhouettes on the screens in the doorways of the box in different colors with different visual effects based on the cycle of predetermined filters in the software. Once viewers had established that the box was an interactive canvas, they were able to place their own images against the physical reality of the iconic box, itself a tool for networking and communicating. The open nature of the piece allows for an endless set of possibilities to animate, but with the viewer in control of the forms in a highly personalized way.

8.7

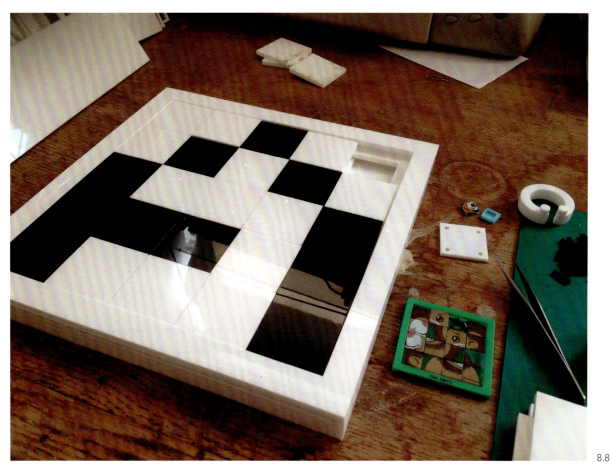

8.8

8.8–8.9
Creator: Ian Mitchell and Sam Meech
Title: TYPuzzle – The Animated Type Maker
Exemplifies: Open Work

The Animated Type Maker (ATM, a deliberate play on Adobe Type Manager) is a system for exhibition visitors to collaborate in the design and production of an animated typeface that is displayed simultaneously in an exhibition and on a large-scale LED window on the exterior of the building. This is done through a tabletop puzzle game consisting of sliding black and white tiles, the playing of which is recorded live and turned into animation. The players can finalize each letterform by moving their hand away from the object. This creates the possibility of generating animations while playing the puzzle.
There is no restriction or predetermined set of outcomes or meanings to the images captured by the users. Audience members bring their own meaning and their own interpretation to both the making and the reading of each unit and each animated outcome.

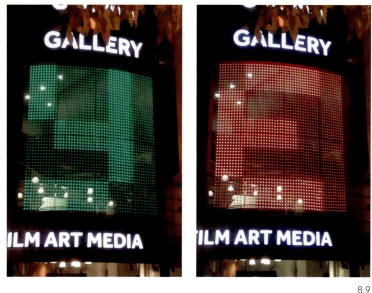

8.9

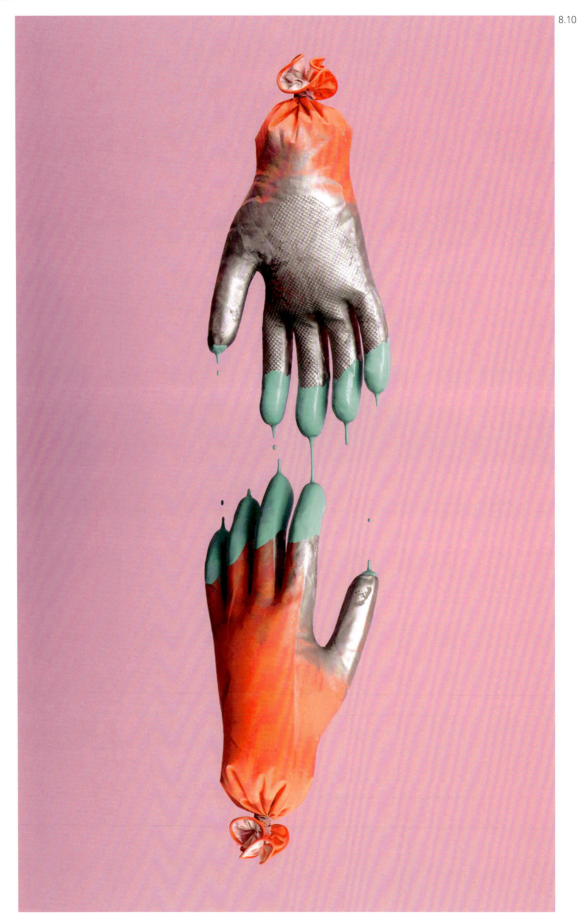

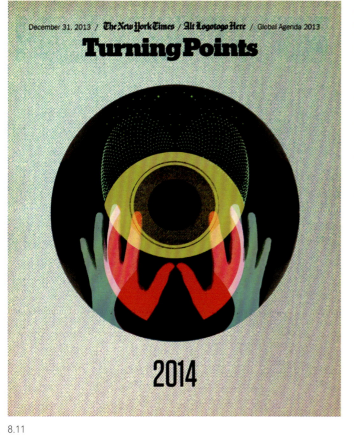

8.11

8.10–8.13
Creator: Jimmy Turrell
Title: Untitled (Various)
Exemplifies: Open Work

These images reprocess imagery from a variety of sources and a variety of periods of design history. Photographs from the early twentieth century are combined with what appear to be mid-century diagrams and pattern. In some cases the images seem religious because of their symmetry and colors, while others are vaguely biological, perhaps even sexual. The act of reading these images is both a challenge and a pleasure as readers are invited to lose themselves in the sensation of the image rather than in a subjective deconstruction of its elements—which is deliberately denied by the open nature of the signifiers.

8.12

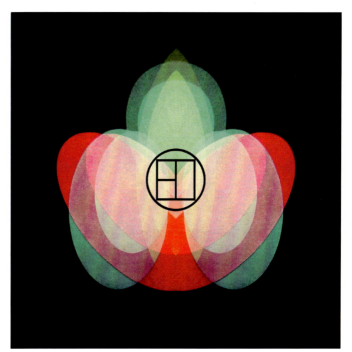

8.13

8.14

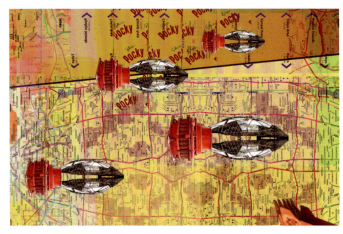

8.15

8.14–8.16
Creator: Kenny Low
**Title: Under the Influence of Little Boy
and Fat Man**
Exemplifies: Open Work

A set of digital panels for an exhibition at
Temasek Polytechnic in Singapore. Each panel is
a rich visual mix of drawings, photographs, and
diagrams from the author's surroundings. The
viewer is plunged into a noisy cityscape with a riot
of color and imagery. Within what appears at first
to be an explosive riot of imagery, you gradually
discern some order within the space around
distinct visual landmarks. Individual elements
reveal themselves from within the dense texture
as recognizable images from the city alongside
influences from other Asian cultures. These, in
turn, are then combined with other signs to form
shapes and meanings that resist a single meaning.
Fragments of architecture are recombined to
resemble a nuclear bomb, and the MRT subway
map is upended and takes on the outline of what
appears to be a jellyfish, in a visual feast that
demands that you spend some time to enjoy the
sensory overload of this graphic metropolis.

Exercises

Exercise 17: Interpretation

There are many different ways to play Telephone—a traditional parlor game. Please use this version as a suggestion only; feel free to adapt it to your own style. You will need a group of people and a way of directing the activity back to the originator. This could be an internet-based game or something much simpler. The objective of this version is to give each participant the opportunity to make an interpretation of what he or she perceives before passing the "message" on to the next person in the chain.

Make an image on a postcard and post it to a friend. Ask that person to translate it into one word and send this word on a postcard to another friend. This recipient should then make an image based on the word and send the image on to be converted into a word, which is then sent on to be made into an image, and so on. The last person in the chain sends the work back to you, completing the circle and signaling that the chain is complete. The postcards should then be brought or sent to a central point for a small exhibition where they are presented in the order they were made.

53. **U. Eco**, *The Open Work* (Hutchinson Radius, 1989; first published 1962).

54. **Zeman**, *"Peirce's Theory of Signs."*

55. **U. Eco**, *The Role of the Reader* (Hutchinson Radius, 1979).

56. **Eco**, *The Open Work*

57. **Eco**, *The Open Work*

Austin, J. L., How to Do Things with Words (Oxford Paperbacks, 1955).

Barthes, R., Elements of Semiology (Cape, 1967).

Barthes, R., Image, Music, Text (Fontana, 1977).

Barthes, R., Mythologies (Paladin, 1972).

Bloomfield, L., Language (George Allen, 1958).

Bolinger, D., Language: The Loaded Weapon (Longman, 1980).

Bourdieu, P., "Intellectual Field and Creative Project" (1966), in Knowledge and Control, edited by M. F. D. Young (Collier-Macmillan, 1971).

Bourdieu, P., Language and Symbolic Power (Polity Press, 1991).

Brake, M., Sociology of Youth Culture and Youth Subcultures (Routledge & Kegan Paul, 1980).

Castleman, C., Getting Up: Subway Graffiti in New York (MIT Press, 1982).

Chafe, W., Meaning and the Structure of Language (University of Chicago Press, 1970).

Culler, J., "Rubbish Theory," in Framing the Sign, edited by J. Culler (Basil Blackwell, 1988).

Douglas, M., Purity and Danger (Routledge & Kegan Paul, 1966).

Eco, U., The Open Work (Hutchinson Radius, 1989; first published 1962).

Eco, U., The Role of the Reader (Hutchinson Radius, 1979).

Foucault, M., The History of Sexuality (Pantheon Books, 1978).

Fuller, M., Flyposter Frenzy (Working Press, 1992).

Galindo, R., "Language Wars: The Ideological Dimensions of the Debates on Bilingual Education," Bilingual Research Journal 21, no. 2–3 (1997): 163–201.

Horn, F. A., Lettering at Work (The Studio Publications, 1955).

Hutchings, R. S., The Western Heritage of Type Design (Cory, Adams and Mackay, 1963).

Jakobson, R., and M. Halle, Fundamentals of Language (Mouton, 1956).

Jefkins, F., Advertisement Writing (MacDonald & Evans Ltd, 1976).

Livingstone, M., Pop Art (Thames & Hudson, 1990).

Manco, T., Stencil Graffiti (Thames & Hudson, 2002).

Marsh, P., E. Rosser, and R. Harré, The Rules of Disorder (Routledge & Kegan Paul, 1977).

McLuhan, M., and Q. Fiore, The Medium Is the Massage: An Inventory of Effects (Allen Lane the Penguin Press, 1967).

Rand, P. A., A Designer's Art (Yale University Press, 1985).

de Saussure, F., Course in General Linguistics (Fontana, 1974; 1st ed. 1915).

Thompson, M., "Rubbish Theory: The Creation and Destruction of Value" (1979), in Framing the Sign, edited by J. Culler (Basil Blackwell, 1988).
UK Office for National Statistics, General Household Survey (1983–86).

Von Bertalanffy, L., General System Theory (George Braziller, Inc., 1968).

Willis, P., Common Culture (Open University Press, 1990).

Wittgenstein, L., Philosophical Investigations (1953), in S. Gablik, Magritte (Thames & Hudson, 1970).

Zeman, J., "Peirce's Theory of Signs," in A Perfusion of Signs, edited by T. Sebeok (Indiana University Press, 1977).

ACKNOWLEDGMENTS AND CREDITS

Visual Curation by Seel Garside, without whom this book would not have been possible.

Special thanks to Wendy, Ailsa, George and Martha Crow. Thank you to Lynsey Brough and Claire Henry at Bloomsbury Publishing, Chris Black at Lachina and all my colleagues at Manchester School of Art for their encouragement, patience and support.

Picture credits

p7 Courtesy of Michael O'Shaughnessy

p10 Courtesy of Dylan Fox

p12-13 Courtesy of Michael O'Shaughnessy

p18 Courtesy of Seel Garside

p19 Pictogram-me, Bergen Academy of Art and Design

p20 © ADAGP, Paris and DACS, London 2015

p21 © DACS 2015

p23 Courtesy of Emily Alston

pp24-25 Courtesy of Dorothy

pp26-27 Courtesy of Hans van Halem

pp28-29 Courtesy of Kollektiv Migrantas

p30 Courtesy of Matt Varker

p32 Courtesy of Seel Garside

p37 [2.2] Courtesy of Emily Alston

p37 [2.3] Courtesy of David Shrigley

p39 Courtesy of Emily Alston

p44 Courtesy of David Crow

p45 [2.6] Courtesy of Seel Garside

p47 Courtesy of David Crow

pp48-49 Courtesy of Dorothy

pp50-51 All designs by Jason Munn

pp52-53 Courtesy of Sarah Illenberger

pp54-55 Courtesy of PHUNK

p56 Design by Dan Funderburgh; printed by Flavorpaper

p58 Courtesy of Sam Harris

pp65-66 Green Man 2014 – Character illustration by Nous Vous

pp69 Courtesy of Seel Garside

pp70-71 Courtesy of Sagmeister and Walsh

pp72-72 Courtesy of Jon McNaught

pp74-75 Dream, 2005 and Liberté, 2005 – Realised in the context of the type workshop 'Manual Pixelism', held by Underware at the ECAL Lausanne, January 2005.

pp76-78 © Joe Magee www.periphery.co.uk

p80 Courtesy of Michael O'Shaughnessy

p82 Courtesy of Jas Bachu

p83 Photos courtesy of Alan Sams

p84 Courtesy of Paul Davis

p85 Courtesy of Alan Murphy (personal work)

p88 Loomus, written and drawn by Stephen Appleby, has appeared in The Guardian since 2005.

p89 All published in The Guardian review section. Courtesy of Tom Gauld.

pp90-91 Courtesy of John Hewitt

pp92-93 © Julia Midgley

p94 Courtesy of Paul Davis

p96 Courtesy of David Crow

pp116-117 Courtesy of PHUNK

pp118-119 Courtesy of Jonathan Hitchen

p120 Ecology of Colour – Collaboration between Nous Vous and Studio Weave for Artlands, North Ken. Photo by Jim Stephenson.

p121 Project commissioned by The Everyman Theatre, Liverpool and Uniform Creative Consultancy <uniform.net>

pp122-123 Courtesy of Jimmy Turrell

p124 Courtesy of Katy Dawkins

p126 Courtesy of Kay Dale

p128 Courtesy of James Jarvis

p129 Courtesy of James Gosnold

p131 Courtesy of David Crow

p132 Courtesy of Ian Wright

pp134-135 Courtesy of Supermundane/Rob Lowe

p136-137 © Kate Moross

pp138-139 Courtesy of Designers Republic/ Manchester School of Art

pp140-141 Illustrations by Ben Jones, Jon Spencer, Chris Rodenhurst and Seel Garside as part of LJMU project 'I Don't Love Soccer'

p142 Pictogram-me, Bergen and Academy of Art and Design

p144 Courtesy of Jimmy Bentley

p147 Courtesy of Joe Briggs Price and Ian Walker

p148 Courtesy of Jack Hatton

p155 and 156 Courtesy of David Crow

p157 © Succession Marcel Duchamp/ADAGP, Paris and DACS, London 2015

p158-159 Objects made by Hazel Jones. Photo courtesy of Alan Sams.

p160 Courtesy of David Crow

p161 Courtesy of Rodrigo de Filippis

p162 © Joe Magee www.periphery.co.uk

p164 Courtesy of Seel Garside

p173 Courtesy of Ian Wright

p174 Courtesy of Seel Garside

p178 Courtesy of Emily Forgot

p179 Edward Carvalho Monaghan

p180 Courtesy of David Crow with Media LAB

p181 Courtesy of Ian Mitchell

pp182-183 Courtesy of Jimmy Turrell

pp184-186 © 2014, Kenny Low